DATE DUE

The Market
for Woodpulp

PRAEGER SPECIAL STUDIES IN
INTERNATIONAL ECONOMICS AND DEVELOPMENT

The Market for Woodpulp

A GLOBAL AND REGIONAL STUDY

R. L. J. Carter

Prepared by
The Economist Intelligence Unit

FREDERICK A. PRAEGER, Publishers
New York · Washington · London

The purpose of the Praeger Special Studies is to make specialized research monographs in U.S. and international economics and politics available to the academic, business, and government communities. For further information, write to the Special Projects Division, Frederick A. Praeger, Publishers, 111 Fourth Avenue, New York, N.Y. 10003.

FREDERICK A. PRAEGER, PUBLISHERS
111 Fourth Avenue, New York, N.Y. 10003, U.S.A.
5, Cromwell Place, London S.W. 7, England

Published in the United States of America in 1968
by Frederick A. Praeger, Inc., Publishers

Library of Congress Catalog Card Number: 68-29312

Printed in the United States of America

CONTENTS

LIST OF TABLES

INTRODUCTION

The principal object of this study is to present, in a concise and readable form, a broad assessment of the past pattern and probable future development of the demand for and supply of woodpulp. The analysis is undertaken both in global and in regional terms, and seeks, inter alia, to quantify the relationship which exists between supply and demand in the seven major geographical regions--Europe, the U.S.S.R., North America, Latin America, Africa, Asia, and the Pacific Area--and to determine the extent and nature of the regional interdependence which exists in the woodpulp sector.

The Food and Agricultural Organisation (FAO) of the United Nations has of course undertaken an enormous amount of research into the field of pulp and paper in recent years, and in view of their extensive coverage and authoritative nature, this study relies heavily on the various statistical series produced by the FAO. Thus, while separate acknowledgements are not made in the text, each of the tables presented in this book is based on original FAO statistics which appear in a number of global and regional studies, and in the Yearbook of Forest Products Statistics.

Throughout this study, all units of weight are expressed in terms of short tons of 2,000 pounds (equivalent to 0.907 metric tons).

The Market
for Woodpulp

CHAPTER 1   THE DERIVED
             DEMAND
             FOR WOODPULP

    Any forward-looking assessment of the world demand for wood-
pulp and the probable development of global and regional production
and trade between the main geographical regions needs to proceed by
means of an analysis of the trend in consumption of the principal end
product.   This chapter is accordingly devoted to a consideration of
the pattern of paper and paperboard usage over the past decade, and
the prospective level of demand in the period up to 1975.   Although
the bulk of the world's woodpulp requirements is a derivative of the
demand for paper and paperboard, relatively small quantities of
dissolving pulp are used in a number of other applications.   In addition, mechanical pulp is used in the manufacture of fibreboard,
although production is carried on mainly by the sawmilling sector in
an integrated operation based largely on raw material yielded from
the industry's principal activity.   As a pulp-based product, however,
fibreboard not only places a demand upon the world's forest resources,
but also serves to augment the derived demand for woodpulp.   A brief
consideration of current production and future requirements of both
dissolving pulp and fibreboard is accordingly included in this study.

    It is perhaps hardly necessary to stress the economic significance
of paper, paperboard, and converted products.   In newspapers, books,
and periodicals; writing papers; in countless types of packaging; in
household and sanitary uses; and in an enormous range of industrial
applications these products have become essential to everyday life.
The level of per capita consumption of paper (including paperboard
and converted products) is indeed a fairly accurate indication of the
relative stage of advancement through which any particular economy
is passing.   There is, accordingly, a marked and positive relationship between the demand for paper and paperboard and income growth,
with per capita consumption being very much higher in the industrialised or developed countries than in the less economically advanced
regions.   As large areas of the world--containing perhaps three
quarters or more of the world's population--are still in the early
stages of their economic development, it is clear that increasingly
extensive demands will be placed in future years on the world's papermaking facilities, and on the resources of the pulp-producing regions
in particular.

1

During the course of the ten years up to 1964, demand showed
astounding growth. Aggregate world consumption of paper and paperboard rose from 56. 7 to 101. 5 million tons, or by nearly 80 per cent
in that period. This represents an average annual rate of growth of
around 6 per cent, which is very considerably faster than the increase
--averaging about 2 per cent per annum--which has taken place in the
world's population. Within these aggregate figures, it is possible to
differentiate between two major categories of paper and paperboard.
First, there are the cultural papers, which can be further divided into
newsprint and other printing and writing papers. The second category
embraces the industrial papers, which include all other types of paper
and paperboard, the large bulk of which are used in a wide range of
packaging applications.

As far as newsprint is concerned, consumption has grown from
11. 5 million tons in 1954 to 18. 1 million tons in 1964, which represents
an aggregate increase of nearly 58 per cent. It is noticeable, however, that the expansion in newsprint consumption has been significantly slower than the growth which has taken place in consumption of
paper and paperboard as a whole. As a result, the share of newsprint in total paper and paperboard consumption has fallen slightly,
from 20. 2 per cent in 1954 to 17. 8 per cent in 1964. In the case of
the remaining sector of the cultural paper category--other printing and
writing papers--consumption rose between 1954 and 1964 from 10. 3 to
18. 8 million tons, representing a rate of expansion virtually the same
as that achieved by consumption of paper and paperboard as a whole.
Under the impact of the much slower rate of growth in newsprint consumption, however, cultural papers as a group have formed a declining proportion of aggregate paper and paperboard consumption in
recent years.

Cultural papers are unlike other categories of paper and paperboard. They are not exposed to any direct competition from other
materials in the majority of their applications, since paper is
effectively the only material which can be used to print or write on.
Competition is of course experienced from other communication
media, notably radio and television, and normally intensifies with
the growth of advertising in developed economies. In the main, however, the slower advance of cultural papers within the total level of
paper and paperboard consumption over the past decade reflects the
approach to saturation level in a number of the more advanced nations
as far as newsprint consumption is concerned, and the relatively low
level, and slow advance, of literacy and income throughout large
areas of the world. Since North America and Europe account for such
a huge proportion of total consumption of cultural papers, it is difficult
at present consumption levels for any slackening in the growth of usage

in these two regions to be offset by an appropriate rate of expansion
in the remaining areas of the world.

As the increase in consumption of cultural papers has failed to
match the rate of growth in consumption of paper and paperboard as
a whole, it is clear that the most dynamic part of the market is to be
found in the industrial paper and paperboard sector.   The expansion
in the use of these grades has continued at a very rapid pace in
recent years; consumption has, in fact, nearly doubled during the
decade under consideration, rising from 34. 9 to 64. 7 million tons.
Owing to this above-average growth, the share of total consumption
accounted for by industrial paper and paperboard has risen from
61. 6 per cent in 1954 to 63. 7 per cent in 1964.

A large proportion of industrial papers and paperboards are
used in a variety of packaging applications, and the major factor
contributing to this group's advance in recent years stems of course
from the growing importance acquired by packaging in countries with
developed economies.   It is for this reason that so much of the
global consumption of industrial paper and paperboard is accounted
for by the North American and European regions.   Moreover,
demand for industrial paper and paperboard tends to be better
sustained at higher levels of income than does consumption of
cultural papers.   In short, therefore, North America and Europe
are such large users that even small changes in their consumption
of paper and paperboard--especially of the major categories--can
be seen in the pattern of consumption in the world as a whole.

TABLE 1

Global and Regional Consumption of Paper and Paperboard

	Volume ('000 tons)		Percentage Increase	Percentage Share	
	1954	1964	1954-64	1954	1964
Europe	15,277	30,033	97	27.0	29.6
U.S.S.R.	2,645	4,539	72	4.7	4.5
North America	31,873	46,997	47	56.2	46.3
Latin America	1,692	3,511	107	3.0	3.4
Africa	525	1,260	140	0.9	1.2
Asia	3,914	13,785	252	6.9	13.6
Pacific Area	746	1,398	87	1.3	1.4
World Total	56,672	101,523	79	100.0	100.0

Thus in 1964, North America and Europe together accounted for rather more than three quarters of total world consumption of paper and paperboard.   It is noticeable, however, that in North America the rate of expansion which has been achieved in recent years has been little more than half that recorded by world consumption as a whole.   As a result, North America's share of total consumption of paper and paperboard has fallen quite appreciably, from 56.2 per cent in 1954 to 46.3 per cent in 1964.   In spite of this trend, however, the sheer volume of North American consumption, while not quite dwarfing that of the rest of the world, certainly has a marked influence on global trends.   Thus, even at this relatively low rate of advance, annual consumption of paper and paperboard in North America still increased by more than 15 million tons over the decade, in comparison with a global expansion of about three times this magnitude.

While Europe uses considerably less paper and paperboard than North America, both in aggregate and in per capita terms, Table 1 reveals that an almost comparable increase (of 14.8 million tons) took place in Europe between 1954 and 1964, which served nearly to double the level of consumption.   In North America, on the other hand, such an absolute increase in consumption represented a proportionate expansion of just under half this amount.

In the U.S.S.R., the rate of growth in consumption has been somewhat below the average world level, largely due to the emphasis which has been put on agriculture and heavy industry during this period, with a consequent restraint placed on consumption goods, including paper.   But the U.S.S.R. apart, each of the four remaining geographical regions has increased its demand for paper and paperboard at rates above (and, in the case of Africa and Asia in particular, well above) the world average over the 1954-64 decade. Being, in the main, a relatively developed area with a fairly high average per capita level of paper consumption, the Pacific Area's growth between 1954 and 1964 was not significantly different from the aggregate world figure.   In Latin America and Africa, small increases were recorded in their respective shares of global consumption between 1954 and 1964.   The most dramatic expansion, however, has been achieved in Asia, largely reflecting the rapid upsurge which has taken place in Japan.   Consumption in this region expanded by over 250 per cent in the ten years up to 1964, with the result that Asia has almost doubled its share of world consumption.

In general, therefore, consumption of paper and paperboard in the developing regions over the past decade has proceeded at a

TABLE 2

Global and Regional Consumption of the Major Categories of Paper and Paperboard ('000 tons)

	1954				1964			
	News-Print	Other Printing and Writing Papers	Other Paper and Paperboard	Total	News-Print	Other Printing and Writing Papers	Other Paper and Paperboard	Total
Europe	2,865	3,410	9,002	15,277	4,997	6,516	18,520	30,033
U.S.S.R.	364	593	1,688	2,645	618	998	2,923	4,539
North America	6,507	5,057	20,291	31,873	8,617	8,236	30,144	46,997
Latin America	482	288	922	1,692	822	549	2,140	3,511
Africa	96	107	322	525	291	239	730	1,260
Asia	851	743	2,320	3,914	2,255	2,060	9,470	13,785
Pacific Area	293	97	356	746	472	192	734	1,398
World Total	11,458	10,313	34,901	56,672	18,072	18,790	64,661	101,523

5

faster pace than in North America and Europe. The former have
consequently raised their combined share of global consumption
quite significantly, from under 18 per cent in 1954 to nearly one
quarter in 1964. In absolute terms, however, it is interesting to
note that the increase in world consumption of paper and paperboard
of around 45 million tons which took place during this period was
divided almost equally among North America, Europe, and the rest
of the world.

As far as production of paper and paperboard is concerned, the
predominance of the two main consuming regions is even more
marked, since North America and Europe both produce a sizable
volume of paper and paperboard surplus to their requirements. Thus
in 1964, these two regions accounted for 78.7 per cent of global production, compared with 75.8 per cent of world consumption. It is
noticeable, however, that not only has the relative predominance of
these two regions both as producers and as users of paper and paperboard declined during the decade under consideration--since in 1954
North America and Europe accounted for a combined share of global
production and consumption of 86.7 per cent and 83.2 per cent,
respectively--but, equally interesting, the differential between these
two proportions has also fallen, signifying that the relative importance
of Europe and North America as net exporters to the rest of the world
has fallen. In other words, the remaining regions of the world as
a whole have been successful in lessening the extent of their dependence on imports from outside sources, and have been supplying a
growing proportion of their own requirements of paper and paperboard.
This expansion has not all been based on a comparable increase in
availabilities of indigenous fibrous raw materials. Nevertheless,
it is evident that over the past ten years or so there has been a
slight trend towards a decentralisation of the world's paper industry.

Looking at the regions individually, we find that North America
is the only one where the rate of increase in production of paper and
paperboard has lagged behind the world average during the decade
under consideration. As a result, North America's share of world
output has fallen quite steeply from 57.7 per cent in 1954 to 48.5 per
cent in 1964. Europe, on the other hand, has increased its share of
global production slightly from 29.0 to 30.2 per cent, while the
U.S.S.R. has just maintained its relative position, its output having
advanced at virtually the same rate as the world total.

In each of the four remaining regions output has advanced at
rates between nearly two and four times greater than that achieved
by global production, with the most rapid expansion--of around

TABLE 3

Global and Regional Production of Paper and Paperboard

	Volume ('000 tons)		Percentage Increase	Percentage Share	
	1954	1964	1954-64	1954	1964
Europe	16,515	30,749	86	29.0	30.2
U.S.S.R.	2,550	4,543	78	4.5	4.5
North America	32,863	49,373	50	57.7	48.5
Latin America	1,029	2,473	140	1.8	2.4
Africa	190	722	280	0.3	0.7
Asia	3,385	12,884	281	6.0	12.6
Pacific Area	391	1,074	175	0.7	1.1
World Total	56,923	101,818	79	100.0	100.0

Note: The above figures of world production of paper and paperboard differ slightly from those shown in Tables 1 and 2 in respect of world consumption. The latter represent the aggregate of each region's production, plus imports, less exports, but, due largely to the leads and lags of international trade, recorded world exports in any given year are invariably in excess of recorded world imports. As a result, world consumption calculated on this basis tends to fall some way short of world production.

280 per cent--occurring in the Asian and African regions. In absolute terms, however, the expansion was very considerably greater in Asia. There, it represented an increase in annual output of some 9.5 million tons--compared with an expansion in North American production of 16.5 million tons over the same period, and an increase in European output of around 14.2 million tons. Asia has accordingly more than doubled its share of world output--from 6.0 per cent in 1954 to 12.6 per cent in 1964. Latin America, Africa, and the Pacific Area each accounted for a larger share of world output of paper and paperboard in 1964 than in 1954, although, in comparison with the performance of Asia, the increases that have been achieved have been considerably less dramatic in both proportionate and absolute terms.

As noted earlier in this chapter when considering the relative trends in North America and Europe, the remaining regions of the world taken as a whole have tended to reduce their proportionate dependence on net imports from North America and Europe, and

have been providing a growing share of their domestic paper and
paperboard requirements.   This subject is considered in rather
more detail later in this chapter in terms of the significance and
extent of regional net exports and net imports.   At this stage, however, it may be interesting to illustrate this point by comparing the
proportionate rate of increase in production and consumption of paper
and paperboard between 1954 and 1964 in the five deficit regions,
i. e. those where consumption was in excess of production during this
period.

	Percentage Increase in Production of Paper and Paperboard 1954-64	Percentage Increase in Consumption of Paper and Paperboard 1954-64
U. S. S. R.	78	72
Latin America	140	107
Africa	280	140
Asia	281	252
Pacific Area	175	87
Total	188	157

     As the table shows, production of paper and paperboard in these
regions between 1954 and 1964 grew faster than consumption.   This
signifies a general decline in their combined proportionate dependence
on net imported supplies (although, as discussed subsequently, with
the exception of the Pacific Area net imports into all these regions
in absolute terms have been rising in recent years).   This relative
decline was particularly marked in Africa and the Pacific Area, with
both of these regions achieving a rate of expansion in production of
paper and paperboard twice as great as the increase in consumption.
A less sizable, but still significant reduction in the dependence on
net imports occurred in Latin America and also in Asia.   In fact,
Asia is the least dependent (in proportionate rather than absolute
terms) of these four regions on net imports of paper and paperboard.
Finally, in the U. S. S. R. consumption of paper and paperboard was
somewhat in excess of production in 1954, but by 1964 this situation
had been reversed and a small net exportable surplus had consequently
been achieved.

     The general development of world exports of paper and paper-
board over the past decade is outlined in Table 4.   During this
period, world exports increased from just under 10 million tons to
rather more than 17 million tons.   This represents an expansion of
just over 70 per cent, compared with an expansion in global output over the same years of 79 per cent.   This signifies that a

TABLE 4

Global and Regional Exports of Paper and Paperboard

	Volume ('000 tons)		Percentage Share	
	1954	1964	1954	1964
Europe	3,556	7,591	35.6	44.6
U.S.S.R.	65	194	0.7	1.1
North America	6,211	8,664	62.2	50.9
Latin America	3	44	-	0.2
Africa	30	69	0.3	0.4
Asia	121	319	1.2	1.9
Pacific Area	3	148	-	0.9
World Total	9,989	17,029	100.0	100.0

rather smaller proportion of output was moving into international trade in 1964 (16.7 per cent) than in 1954 (17.5 per cent).   On the face of it the relative decline in trade seems surprising.   Very large disparities in consumption exist between the developed and the developing regions of the world, and there is no real pressure on the productive resources of the former at existing consumption levels.   What is the explanation?   Evidently the diminution in the relative importance of international trade may be taken as a reflection of the developing regions' efforts to conserve foreign exchange earnings by restraining imports of paper and paperboard and at the same time expanding their domestic papermaking capacity.

The predominant position of North America and Europe as world exporters of paper and paperboard can be readily seen from the above table.   Between them, these two regions accounted for a combined share of 97.8 per cent of total exports in 1954 and 95.5 per cent in 1964.   Within these totals, however, the relative importance of North America has fallen significantly.   In 1964 the region accounted for only 50.9 per cent of world exports of paper and paperboard compared with 62.2 per cent in 1954.   On the other hand, Europe's share has risen by almost as much as North America's share has fallen.

As far as the individual categories of paper and paperboard are concerned, newsprint accounts for a considerably larger share of total exports than its significance in world output suggests.   Thus in 1954, newsprint output represented 20.2 per cent of global production of all grades of paper and paperboard, yet newsprint accounted for as much as 68.8 per cent of world trade.   By 1964, however, these proportions had both fallen slightly,to 17. 7 per cent and 55. 3 per cent, respectively.

The major contribution made by newsprint to trade reflects the fact that it is a standardised product used in large quantities and capable of being made with very substantial economies of scale if the mill is located near the source of raw materials rather than, as an alternative, close to its final market.   At the same time, however, the slight decline which has taken place in the prominence of newsprint in global exports reflects the growing importance of other categories of paper--and industrial paper and paperboard in particular--in aggregate consumption.   In addition, a trend towards the regional specialisation of production in the face of a growing range of individual grades has tended to promote international trade in grades other than newsprint.

A consideration of the regional pattern of imports of all categories of paper and paperboard again reveals the dominant position of North America and Europe.   The proportion of global imports accounted for by these two regions, however, is somewhat less than in the case of world exports of paper and paperboard, with the difference representing the extent to which they supply a net exportable surplus to other parts of the world.

TABLE 5

Global and Regional Imports of Paper and Paperboard

	Volume ('000 tons)		Percentage Share	
	1954	1964	1954	1964
Europe	2,318	6,875	23.8	41.1
U.S.S.R.	160	190	1.6	1.1
North America	5,221	6,288	53.6	37.6
Latin America	666	1,082	6.8	6.5
Africa	365	607	3.8	3.6
Asia	650	1,220	6.7	7.3
Pacific Area	358	472	3.7	2.8
World Total	9,738	16,734	100.0	100.0

Note: The total world import figures shown above differ slightly from the world export figures set out in Table 4, due largely to the fact that the leads and lags of international trade normally result in a higher level of recorded exports than recorded imports in any given year.

The relative importance of North America as an export market has declined quite sharply during the decade under consideration. In 1954, this region accounted for over half (53. 6 per cent) of world imports of paper and paperboard, but by 1964 its share had fallen by nearly one third to 37. 6 per cent.   Europe, on the other hand, has become a very much more sizable importer.   The volume of imports into Europe in 1954 was well under half of that entering the North American market, but while imports into the latter rose by just over 1 million tons during the following ten years, European imports nearly trebled, increasing by more than 4. 5 million tons. As a result, by 1964 Europe had assumed North America's original position as the largest regional import market for paper and paper- board.

On balance, the relative importance of the remaining five geographical regions taken as a whole has remained largely unchanged--in 1954 they accounted for 21. 3 per cent of world imports compared with 22. 6 per cent in 1954.   Within this total, however, the share in total imports accounted for by the U. S. S. R. , Latin America, Africa, and the Pacific Area has fallen, and only Asia has increased its relative importance as an export market.

Having discussed the regional pattern of both exports and imports of paper and paperboard, it may now be interesting to consider briefly the development of net regional trade between 1954 and 1964.

A number of interesting trends are revealed by the statistics in the following table.   As far as the net exporting regions are concerned, the relative importance of North America has increased very significantly.   During the decade under consideration, the excess of exports over imports of paper and paperboard was rising from just under 1 million tons in 1954 to nearly 2. 4 million tons in 1964.   The volume of European net exports, on the other hand, has fallen quite steeply from 1. 2 to 0. 7 million tons over this period, while the U. S. S. R. , which in 1954 was a fairly small net importer of paper and paperboard, had by 1964 developed a modest net export- able surplus.

Within the aggregate volume of North American net exports of paper and paperboard, there has been a particularly marked expan- sion in industrial grades, with net exports rising by over 1 million tons between 1954 and 1964.   This represents a rather more than fourfold expansion, while net exports of newsprint and other printing and writing papers, on the other hand, have risen by only around 50 per cent.   In Europe, however, the net exportable surplus of

TABLE 6

Net Regional Trade in Paper and Paperboard ('000 tons)

	1954				1964			
	News-Print	Other Printing and Writing Papers	Other Paper and Paperboard	Total	News-Print	Other Printing and Writing Papers	Other Paper and Paperboard	Total
Europe	+289	+327	+622	+1,238	+213	+451	+ 52	+ 716
U.S.S.R.	+ 34	- 53	- 76	- 95	+ 80	- 70	- 6	+ 4
North America	+671	+ 64	+255	+ 990	+981	+100	+1,295	+2,376
Latin America	-425	- 84	-154	- 663	-579	- 94	- 365	-1,038
Africa	- 96	- 63	-176	- 335	-175	-101	- 262	- 538
Asia	-193	- 67	-269	- 529	-386	- 48	- 467	- 901
Pacific Area	-214	- 63	- 78	- 355	-162	- 73	- 89	- 324

Note: A plus sign indicates net exports and a minus sign net imports. Due to the leads and lags of international trade, however, which result in a difference between the volume of exports and imports recorded in any given year, the sums in the above columns do not balance precisely.

industrial paper and paperboard fell sharply from 622,000 to 52,000 tons between 1954 and 1964, while net exports of newsprint also diminished, although much less markedly.   These declines were partially offset, however, by an increase in the volume of net exports of printing and writing papers other than newsprint.

As far as the U.S.S.R. is concerned, it is interesting to note that net exports of newsprint have been sufficiently developed over the 1954-64 period, and the reliance on net imports of other categories of paper and paperboard sufficiently reduced, to yield a slight over-all net exportable surplus in 1964, compared with a net deficit of 95,000 tons in 1954.   Latin America and Asia have each increased their net reliance on outside supplies in absolute terms quite substantially between 1954 and 1964. The Pacific Area's volume of net imports, however, has fallen slightly over this period.

For the four geographical regions which were net importers of paper and paperboard in 1964, the figures in Table 7 illustrate the trend noted earlier in this chapter in respect of their diminishing reliance, in proportionate terms, on net imports.

In total, the proportion of aggregate paper and paperboard consumption accounted for by net imports in the four deficit regions fell by almost one half between 1954 and 1964, from 27.4 per cent to 14.0 per cent.   In Asia, dependence on net imports of paper and paperboard was reduced by more than 50 per cent over this period, and a comparable achievement was recorded by the Pacific Area. Reduced reliance on net imports during this decade was less sizable in the remaining two regions, amounting to around one quarter in Latin America and one fifth in Africa.   Yet the dependence of each region on outside supplies of paper and paperboard still remained very considerable in 1964, representing 29.6 per cent and 42.7 per cent, respectively, of the regional volume of consumption.

As discussed subsequently in Chapter 3, a somewhat greater dependence on net imports is revealed in certain of these regions once inter-regional trade in papermaking grades of woodpulp is brought into the picture.   For the present, however, it may now be appropriate to consider briefly recent and projected future trends in the demand for dissolving pulp and fibreboard before passing onto an analysis of the expected level of consumption of paper and paperboard in 1975.

The largest single outlet for dissolving pulp is of course in the production of rayon for use in textiles and tyre cords.   Although it

TABLE 7

The Deficit Regions' Dependence on Net Imports of Paper and Paperboard ('000 tons)

	1954			1964		
	Consumption	Net Imports	Net Imports as Percentage of Consumption	Consumption	Net Imports	Net Imports as Percentage of Consumption
Latin America	1,692	663	39.2	3,511	1,038	29.6
Africa	525	335	63.8	1,260	538	42.7
Asia	3,914	529	13.5	13,785	901	6.5
Pacific Area	746	355	47.6	1,398	324	23.2
	6,877	1,882	27.4	19,954	2,801	14.0

has numerous other applications--it is used, for example, in the manufacture of such products as cellophane, plastics, solvents, explosives, and varnishes--the future trend in output of dissolving pulp is expected to continue to be very largely determined by the demand for rayon.

In both its principal applications--textiles and tyre cords--dissolving pulp is facing keen competition from the newer synthetics. As a result, consumption is expected to expand only moderately in those countries which are currently the most important consumers--the United States, Japan, and the U.K.--but to grow at a somewhat faster rate in Eastern Europe and in the U.S.S.R. in particular. In the developing countries where the newer synthetics are not produced it is also considered that the demand for rayon will be rather more dynamic. The slow rate of expansion in demand in the countries which currently account for the bulk of global consumption of dissolving pulp, however, will be the main determinant of the over-all trend. Hence it is judged that by 1975 dissolving pulp will tend to form an even smaller part of world output of woodpulp than the share of around 5 per cent which it made up in the early 1960's.

The FAO accordingly estimates that regional and global consumption of dissolving pulp will develop along the following lines in the period up to 1975.

TABLE 8

Actual and Estimated Consumption of Dissolving Woodpulp

	Volume ('000 tons)		Percentage Increase
	1960-62	1975	1960-62 to 1975
Europe	1,776	2,400	35
U.S.S.R.	206	1,210	487
North America	1,204	1,420	18
Latin America	71	100	41
Africa)			
Asia)	764	1,270	66
Pacific Area)			
World Total	4,021	6,400	59

The third component of aggregate demand for woodpulp is formed by fibreboard, a panel material of which there are two main types--compressed (hardboard) and non-compressed (insulation board). Hardboard is used mainly for exterior siding, subflooring,

wall surfacing, door facing, and concrete formwork, but considerable quantities are also used in the furniture and other woodworking
industries.   Non-compressed fibreboard, or insulation board, is
used largely for sheathing and interior furnishing for temperature
and sound insulation.

Fibreboard is invariably produced in an integrated operation by
the sawmilling industry using raw material which is often a by-
product of its principal activity.   Hence in this respect fibreboard
is unlike paper in that the provision of market pulp is not an important feature of the industry.   It is nevertheless a pulp-based product
and as such is included in this study.   Not only does it serve to
place an additional demand upon the world's forest resources, but
it also competes directly with the pulp and paper industry in terms
of the size and type of wood required.

The trend in global and regional output of fibreboard between
1954 and 1964 is set out in the following table:

TABLE 9

Global and Regional Production of Fibreboard

	Volume ('000 tons)		Percentage Increase	Percentage Share	
	1954	1964	1954-64	1954	1964
Europe	1,177	2,696	129	37.8	41.8
U.S.S.R.	58	413	612	1.9	6.4
North America	1,657	2,483	50	53.2	38.5
Latin America	29	141	386	0.9	2.2
Africa	44	141	220	1.4	2.2
Asia	37	385	941	1.2	6.0
Pacific Area	114	186	63	3.6	2.9
World Total	3,116	6,445	107	100.0	100.0

Global output of fibreboard rather more than doubled between
1954 and 1964, rising from 3.1 to 6.4 million tons.   As with other
woodpulp products, the world's industry is dominated by North
America and Europe.   With the sharp upsurge in manufacturing
capacity in most other regions, however, the combined share of
total output accounted for by North America and Europe has tended
to decline, falling from 91 per cent in 1954 to just over 80 per cent
in 1964.   While North American output of fibreboard rose by only
50 per cent over this period, production in Europe rose at a rate

some two and a half times faster.   As a result, European output in
1964 was well in excess of the North American level of production.

During the decade under consideration, there has been a tendency
for a growing proportion of fibreboard output to find its way into
international trade.   In 1954, world exports of fibreboard represented
about 15 per cent of aggregate production, but by 1964 this proportion
had risen to nearly 20 per cent.   As can be seen from the following
table, Europe is easily the largest exporter of fibreboard, and
accounted for well over 80 per cent of global exports in both 1954 and
1964.   It is also the principal importing region, although imports
tend to be at a somewhat lower level than exports.   Europe is
accordingly the main net exporting region, while North America, in
spite of the fact that it accounted for 38.5 per cent of global output
of fibreboard in 1964, is nevertheless the major net importing
region.

TABLE 10

Global and Regional Trade in Fibreboard ('000 tons)

	Exports		Imports		Net Trade	
	1954	1964	1954	1964	1954	1964
Europe	408	1,032	292	852	+116	+180
U.S.S.R.	-	36	-	1	-	+ 35
North America	42	73	71	241	- 29	-168
Latin America	-	19	19	10	- 19	+ 9
Africa	17	58	20	37	- 3	+ 21
Asia	2	8	30	58	- 28	- 50
Pacific Area	3	31	3	4	-	+ 27
World Total	472	1,257	435	1,203	+ 37	+ 54

Note: A plus sign indicates net exports and a minus sign net
         imports.   Total world exports and imports do not
         balance precisely, however, due to the leads and lags
         of international trade.   Hence the aggregate regional
         net trade figures in the last two columns fail to cancel
         out.

Much of the recent growth in the use of fibreboard and other
wood-based panel products, such as plywood and particle board, has
been due to their increasing substitution for sawnwood.   Partly this
reflects the trend in relative prices, and partly the properties of the
two materials--fibreboard in many ways having proved to be more
desirable than sawnwood in meeting the changing needs of the user

industries and sectors.   While it is probable that the demand for
fibreboard and other wood-based panel products is still in its
expansionary stage, however, the fact that their use has so far
grown largely at the expense of sawnwood must necessarily limit
this growth.   Thus, after a certain stage, the relative importance
of the substitution effect in the growth in consumption of these
products must decline.   The rate of expansion in fibreboard usage
has in fact already slowed down in recent years, largely due to a
levelling off in demand and a general absence of growth for insulation
board in some major consuming countries, such as the United States,
Canada, and Sweden.

These trends are reflected in the recent estimates made by the
FAO of fibreboard consumption in 1975.   Thus, while consumption
rose by some 107 per cent between 1954 and 1964, in the eleven-year
period up to 1975 the expansion is expected to be of the order of 90
per cent.   Easily the fastest rate of growth is being anticipated in
the U.S.S.R., with the largest expansion in absolute terms being
looked for in the European market.

TABLE 11

Estimated Consumption of Fibreboard ('000 tons)

	1954	1964	1975
Europe	1,061	2,516	4,400
U.S.S.R.	58	378	1,980
North America	1,686	2,651	3,410
Latin America	48	132	440
Africa	47	120	340
Asia	65	435)	1,650
Pacific Area	114	159)	
World Total	3,079	6,391	12,220

It is interesting to express the use of fibreboard in woodpulp
equivalent.   If the average mechanical pulp content of one ton of
fibreboard is taken as 0.62 tons, then a global consumption level of
12.2 million tons of fibreboard in 1975 would represent a require-
ment of around 7.6 million tons of mechanical woodpulp.

Returning now to a consideration of the main determinant of
woodpulp requirements, global paper and paperboard consumption
in coming years will be influenced, as in the past, by three principal

factors--per capita income, population, and price relationships.
As far as the latter factor is concerned, the FAO, in preparing its
most recent estimates of the future trend in demand for paper and
paperboard, has assumed that there will be no basic change in the
relationship which prevailed in the period used as a basis for the
analysis between the prices of paper and paperboard and those of
the nearest substitutes.

This assumption may perhaps be questioned in some quarters.
In the field of packaging, paper and paperboard has had to face
significant competitive pressures in recent years from a variety of
plastic materials whose production costs have fallen and could well
fall further relative to paper and paperboard prices. In spite of
this, however, the estimates made by the FAO assume that there
will not be a major shift away from paper and paperboard as a packaging material in the period up to 1975. Underlying this assumption is the fact that the expansion in usage of competing packaging
materials,such as plastics,has tended to be complementary rather
than at the expense of paper and paperboard. The many types and
forms of plastic materials which have been developed in recent
years have in fact contributed heavily to the general extension of
the market for packaging materials as a whole. This is not to deny
that paper and paperboard has lost out to plastic materials in a
number of important applications and outlets in some of the more
advanced economies--for example, in the packaging of fertilizers--
and hence the net effect of competition from plastics has probably
been to retard the growth in usage of paper and paperboard in
packaging to some extent. At the same time, however, the paper
and paperboard industry has developed new packaging outlets, and
the FAO estimates assume that the industry will continue to adapt
itself to quickly changing conditions as it has done successfully
during the recent past.

The second major determinant of the demand for paper and
paperboard is the population factor. In 1964 the world population
amounted to some 3, 286 million, and by 1975 this figure is expected
to rise by around 19 per cent to reach a level of about 3, 907 million.
This does not mean, however, that world production of paper and
paperboard will need to expand by a comparable 19 per cent in order
to maintain regional consumption at the 1964 level--quite apart from
any increase in per capita consumption levels being realised--since
the growth in population anticipated in the period up to 1975 is far
from evenly spread throughout the individual regions. The population of the developing regions, which are currently low-level con-
sumers of paper and paperboard, is growing very much faster than

the population of the more developed areas, as illustrated in the
following table:

TABLE 12

Actual and Estimated Population Levels (millions)

	1964	1975	Percentage Increase 1964-75
Europe	441	467	5.9
U.S.S.R.	228	261	14.5
North America	212	243	14.6
Latin America	234	325	38.9
Africa	304	393	29.3
Asia	1,850	2,198	18.8
Pacific Area	17	20	17.6
World Total	3,286	3,907	18.9

In the most important consuming regions, population growth is
expected to be well below the world average in the period from 1964-
75--as low as 5.9 per cent in Europe, and 14.6 per cent in North
America.   The population of Latin America, on the other hand, is
expected to expand more than twice as fast as the world population,
while the projected growth in Africa is well over half as large again
as the global average.

Once an allowance is made for the varying rates in future population growth envisaged for the individual regions, it may be interesting
to note that merely for per capita consumption levels to be maintained
at their present regional levels, aggregate world demand for paper
and paperboard will rise by nearly one seventh between 1964 and 1975.
In absolute terms, an increase of that order represents an extra
demand of around 14 million tons.   An expansion in world requirements of very much more than this magnitude can of course be
expected, reflecting the impact of the third principal determinant of
demand for paper and paperboard--the income effect.

The importance of the income effect on the future level of demand
for paper and paperboard lies of course in the observed fact that
demand varies not only with changes in income but also according to
the stage through which average per capita income levels are passing
in any particular region.   These correlation factors, furthermore,
are also found to differ between the three main categories of paper
and paperboard--newsprint, other printing and writing papers, and
industrial paper and paperboard.

The existence of a marked positive relationship between per capita income and per capita consumption of paper and paperboard as a whole is shown quite clearly in the following table:

TABLE 13

Estimated Consumption of Paper and Paperboard in 1960-62

Income Level (U.S. $ per head)	Country or Region	Consumption of Paper and Paperboard (tons per '000 capita)
Over 2,000	United States	210.5
1,500-2,000	Canada	138.0
	Northern Europe	114.5
	Pacific Area	86.5
1,000-1,500	U.K. and Ireland	107.8
	EEC	69.7
	Central Europe	39.7
500-1,000	Japan	58.5
	Eastern Europe	29.5
	Southern Africa	23.6
	U.S.S.R.	17.5
300-500	Southeast South America	25.0
	Mexico	17.0
	Northern South America	14.3
	Caribbean	12.2
	Mediterranean Basin	12.2
	Southern Europe	10.8
150-300	Brazil	10.4
	Southwest South America	9.5
	East Asia (excluding Japan)	8.6
	Central America	7.1
	Northern Africa	6.3
	Southwest Asia	2.0
	Arabian Peninsula	0.9
Under 150	China (mainland)	4.1
	Continental Southeast Asia	2.1
	Insular Southeast Asia	2.0
	Eastern Africa	1.4
	South Asia	1.3
	Western Africa	0.9

Although there are some quite large variations in per capita consumption levels within each of the average income groupings considered in Table 13, and also a certain amount of overlapping, the general pattern is nevertheless unmistakeable. Consumption of paper and paperboard per head is very much higher in the more economically advanced and affluent areas. Furthermore, the differential between average per capita consumption of paper and paperboard in the lower and higher income groupings widens progressively at a rate considerably in excess of the proportionate increase in per capita income.

The general nature of the relationship between per capita income and per capita consumption of paper and paperboard is that the "income elasticity" tends to decline as incomes rise. At income levels of about $100 per head, the elasticity of consumption is as high as 2.5 to 3--in other words, a rise in per capita income of 1 per cent leads to an increase in consumption of paper and paperboard of some 2.5 to 3 per cent. At slightly higher income levels of around $200 to $400, however, the income elasticity falls to about 1.5 to 2.5. Thus, in this per capita income band, a rise in income of 1 per cent tends to result in a rise in consumption of around 1.5 to 2.5 per cent. Between the $500 and $1,000 per capita income level the income elasticity is still above unity, but for the United States, with an income per head of well in excess of $2,000, the income elasticity is less than unity. Thus in the United States, an increase in per capita income of 1 per cent leads to a rather less than proportionate increase in consumption per head.

The income elasticity of demand for each of the major categories of paper and paperboard has also been observed to decline with rising incomes, but at varying rates. Thus at low income levels, the income elasticity of demand for cultural papers is higher than that for industrial papers, but at income levels in excess of about $800 per head, the elasticity of demand for industrial paper and paperboard is much higher than that for cultural papers.

As a result, for a given rate of income growth, demand for paper and paperboard rises at a much faster rate in the developing countries where per capita consumption levels are low. But in such countries the greater part of the expansion is, initially at least, usually in cultural papers--particularly where there is an accompanying improvement in literacy rates. In developed regions, however, much of the growth is accounted for by the industrial paper and paperboard category, with a major contribution being made by a rapid expansion in demand for the packaging grades.

TABLE 14

Estimated Global and Regional Consumption of Paper and Paperboard ('000 tons)

	Newsprint		Other Printing and Writing Paper		Other Paper and Paperboard		Total Paper and Paperboard	
	1964	1975	1964	1975	1964	1975	1964	1975
Europe	4,997	8,970	6,516	11,410	18,520	35,400	30,033	55,780
U.S.S.R.	618	1,540	998	3,530	2,923	11,500	4,539	16,570
North America	8,617	10,940	8,236	10,430	30,144	40,780	46,997	62,150
Latin America	822	2,000	549	1,365	2,140	4,235	3,511	7,600
Africa	291	500	239	615	730	1,690	1,260	2,805
Asia	2,255	4,160	2,060	5,990	9,470	21,115	13,785	31,265
Pacific Area	472	880	192	310	734	1,200	1,398	2,390
World Total	18,072	28,990	18,790	33,650	64,661	115,920	101,523	178,560

23

On the basis of such correlation factors, projected rates of
regional per capita economic growth varying between 1.9 per cent
per annum in North America and 4.0 per cent per annum in Europe,
and the population forecasts set out earlier in this chapter, the FAO
has recently estimated that world requirements of paper and paperboard will be of the order of 178.6 million tons in 1975--76 per cent
above the level of consumption in 1964.   Details of these estimates
are set out in Table 14, together with a comparison with the 1964
performance.

In general, these estimates suggest that world consumption of
paper and paperboard will tend to grow somewhat slower in the 1964-
75 period than in the previous ten years.   Thus, between 1954 and
1964 global consumption expanded at an average annual rate of
around 6 per cent, whereas the attainment of a level of consumption
of 178.6 million tons by 1975 implies that growth will proceed in
coming years at an average rate of around 5.3 per cent per annum.

Within these aggregate figures, it is envisaged that the rate of
growth in consumption in each of the principal individual sectors will
decline.   The rate of expansion in newsprint consumption is expected
to fall from about 4.7 per cent between 1954 and 1964 to 4.4 per cent
per annum in the period up to 1975.   The average annual rate of
growth of both other printing and writing papers and industrial paper
and paperboard should be slackening from about 6.2 per cent to nearer
5.3 per cent. On the basis of these estimates, the relative importance of cultural papers will continue to fall, and by 1975 they will
represent barely 35 per cent of the total volume of paper and paperboard consumption, compared with 36.3 per cent in 1964 and 38.4
per cent in 1954.

TABLE 15

Estimated Growth in Consumption of Paper and Paperboard, 1964-75

	Million Tons	Per Cent
Europe	25.7	86
U.S.S.R.	12.0	265
North America	15.2	32
Latin America	4.1	116
Africa	1.5	123
Asia	17.5	117
Pacific Area	1.0	71
World Total	77.0	76

As far as the individual regions are concerned, the sharp variations

in regional rates of growth implied by the FAO estimates are shown
in Table 15.   The future pace of expansion in paper and paperboard
consumption is expected to be very much higher in the developing
regions than in those areas where per capita consumption was already
at a relatively high level in 1964.   In North America, it is expected
that the rate of growth in consumption will be less than half the world
average, while in the next highest consuming regions--Europe and
the Pacific Area--consumption is expected to grow at roughly the
same rate as aggregate global consumption.   At the other extreme,
the effect of a sharp rise in per capita income levels and a high income elasticity of demand is reflected in an anticipated increase in
paper and paperboard consumption in the U.S.S.R. between 1964 and
1975 of around 265 per cent--well over three times as fast as the
rate of growth in world consumption as a whole.   Finally, in Latin
America, Africa,and Asia, consumption is expected to advance at
rates of around half as fast again as global consumption.

In concluding this chapter it may be interesting to note that, in
spite of the much more rapid rate of growth in consumption envisaged
in the low consuming regions in the period up to 1975, the actual gap
between consumption in the developing and the developed parts of the
world will tend to widen appreciably.   The widening is partly due to
the incidence of an above-average expansion in population in these
regions, but mainly due to the low consumption levels currently prevailing.   This is illustrated in the following table, which compares
actual regional per capita consumption levels in 1964 with those
expected to be reached by 1975.

TABLE 16

Actual and Estimated Consumption of Paper and Paperboard
(tons per '000 capita)

	1964	1975	Increase 1964-75
Europe	68	119	51
U.S.S.R.	20	64	44
North America	222	256	34
Latin America	15	23	8
Africa	4	7	3
Asia	7	14	7
Pacific Area	82	120	38
World Average	31	46	15

Thus, although per capita consumption in Africa, the lowest
consuming region, is likely to rise by around 75 per cent compared

with a proportionate increase of less than half this magnitude in North America at the other extreme, the gulf between average per capita consumption of paper and paperboard in these two regions is expected to widen from about 218 to 249 tons per thousand persons between 1964 and 1975. While this book concerns itself only with the problems of the regional supply of and demand for woodpulp during this relatively short period, at some later stage during the present century it may be anticipated that this trend will be reversed, and the more rapid development of the low consuming regions will gradually lead to a narrowing of the present differential. Looking even further ahead, it may therefore be of interest to point out, purely for illustrative purposes, that an increase in per capita consumption throughout the world to the level expected to prevail in North America in 1975 would involve an expansion in world output from around 178 million tons in 1975 to approximately 1 billion tons, without any allowance for further increases in population.

CHAPTER **2** GLOBAL AND
REGIONAL TRENDS
IN PRODUCTION

In the rather more than two decades which have passed since
the end of World War II, output of pulp from the world's forests has
recorded a steady and marked expansion, reflecting a continuing
rise in living standards and the accompanying growth in demand for
both cultural and industrial grades of paper and paperboard, dissolving pulp, and fibreboard.   Looking at the rather shorter period
since 1954, by which time most of the major pulp-producing
countries had completely resumed their normal peacetime economic
activities, production of all papermaking and dissolving grades of
woodpulp has soared from 46.7 million tons to a level of 83.4 million
tons in 1964--representing an average annual rate of growth of
around 6 per cent.   In comparison, the world population has expanded over this period at about one third of this pace, at an average of
some 2 per cent a year.

Although North America has continued to overshadow the production scene, output in this region since 1954 has failed to match
the rate of expansion achieved by world production as a whole.   As
a result, while North America still accounts for well over one half
of the world's output of woodpulp, its share has nevertheless fallen
from about 60 per cent in 1954 to little more than 55 per cent in 1964.
European production, on the other hand, has expanded at almost the
same rate as the world total, and hence the relative importance of
Europe as a producing region has remained virtually unchanged
between 1954 and 1964.   Thus, the combined share of the two main
producing regions in world output has declined by five percentage
points, from 88.6 per cent in 1954 to 83.6 per cent in 1964.

With the exception of the U.S.S.R., each of the remaining regions
recorded a significantly above-average increase in output during this
period.   The fastest growth rate was in fact achieved by Africa, with
production rising by 600 per cent, but this is mainly a reflection of
the very low level of output which prevailed in 1954.   The largest
increase in terms of volume occurred in the Asian region, with production more than trebling between 1954 and 1964.   In so doing, Asian

output has now easily outstripped that of the U.S.S.R.   Furthermore, Asia has nearly doubled its share of world production from
4.4 per cent to 7.9 per cent.   Russia's share, on the other hand,
has been maintained at 5.5 per cent, following an increase in output
of 76 per cent between 1954 and 1964.

TABLE 17

Global and Regional Production of Woodpulp

	Volume ('000 tons)		Percentage Increase	Percentage Share	
	1954	1964	1954-64	1954	1964
Europe	13,391	23,548	76	28.7	28.3
U.S.S.R.	2,583	4,551	76	5.5	5.5
North America	27,931	46,172	53	59.9	55.3
Latin America	312	1,198	284	0.7	1.4
Africa	55	385	600	0.1	0.5
Asia	2,049	6,623	223	4.4	7.9
Pacific Area	335	914	173	0.7	1.1
World Total	46,656	83,391	79	100.0	100.0

Within these aggregate figures of world output of woodpulp, however,
there has been an increasing shift in emphasis towards chemical
pulp grades and away from mechanical pulp.   Thus between 1954
and 1964, world production of chemical woodpulp rose by 96 per
cent, while the expansion in output achieved by mechanical pulp has
been less than half this magnitude, amounting to only 45 per cent.
As a result, the proportion of aggregate woodpulp output accounted
for by mechanical grades has shown a marked decline, falling from
34.1 per cent in 1954 to 31.5 per cent in 1959 and to 27.7 per cent
in 1964.   In general, this reflects the fact that growth has taken
place mainly in the industrial and packaging sector, as opposed to
the cultural sector where the bulk of mechanical pulp is used.

TABLE 18

Global Production of Chemical and Mechanical Woodpulp

	Total Woodpulp '000 tons	Chemical Grades		Mechanical Grades	
		'000 tons	Percentage Share	'000 tons	Percentage Share
1954	46,656	30,756	65.9	15,900	34.1
1959	60,484	41,424	68.5	19,060	31.5
1964	83,391	60,259	72.3	23,132	27.7

Looking first at the chemical woodpulp supply situation, both
North America and Europe have lost ground somewhat to the other
producing areas in recent years.   Nevertheless, these two regions
still accounted for 86.5 per cent of total world production of all
grades of chemical woodpulp in 1964, although this compared with
a share of nearly 89 per cent in 1954 (and as much as 91 per cent
three years earlier).

The largest gain in terms of market shares in chemical woodpulp production has been achieved by the Asian region, which
accounted for 8.5 per cent of total world output in 1964 compared
with only 4.1 per cent in 1954.   The expansion in Russia, on the
other hand, has proceeded at well below the pace of world production,
and hence this region's share of the world total has fallen from 6.0
per cent in 1954 to 5.4 per cent in 1964.   In the three remaining
regions--Latin America, Africa,and the Pacific Area--an extremely
rapid rate of growth has been achieved over this period, with the
Pacific Area trebling output, Latin America increasing it fourfold,
and Africa virtually sixfold.   In general, however, these extremely
sharp rates of growth simply reflect abnormally low levels of output
in 1954.   In spite of the dramatic expansion over this decade, the
combined share of these three regions in world output of chemical
woodpulp amounted,in fact,to only 2.6 per cent in 1964.

TABLE 19

Global and Regional Production of Chemical Woodpulp

	Volume ('000 tons)		Percentage Increase	Percentage Share	
	1954	1964	1954-64	1954	1964
Europe	8,507	16,011	88	27.7	26.6
U.S.S.R.	1,853	3,234	75	6.0	5.4
North America	18,760	34,305	83	61.0	56.9
Latin America	158	795	403	0.5	1.3
Africa	52	349	571	0.2	0.6
Asia	1,272	5,108	302	4.1	8.5
Pacific Area	154	457	197	0.5	0.7
World Total	30,756	60,259	96	100.0	100.0

In mechanical pulp,too, the relative importance of North America
as a producing region has tended to diminish in recent years, although
it still dominates the scene by accounting for over half of world output.
Production of mechanical grades of woodpulp in North America during

the years from 1954 to 1964 increased by only 29 per cent.   This
was in the context of a global expansion in output of 45 per cent, however, and hence North America's share has accordingly dropped
quite significantly during this period from nearly 58 per cent to just
over 51 per cent.

All of the other regions have achieved an increase in their shares
of world output of mechanical woodpulp, with Europe recording the
largest gain--its share rising from 30. 7 to 32. 6 per cent between
1954 and 1964.   Elsewhere, the most notable expansion in absolute
terms has taken place in Asia, where output has risen by 95 per cent,
and the region's share of global production has grown from 4. 9 per
cent in 1954 to 6. 5 per cent in 1964.   This rate of expansion has
enabled Asia to maintain and, in fact, slightly extend its lead over the
U. S. S. R. , whose share of world output has risen from 4. 6 per cent
to 5. 7 per cent over this period.

Latin America, Africa, and the Pacific Area accounted for a
combined share of 3. 9 per cent of world output in 1964, compared
with 2. 1 per cent in 1954.

TABLE 20

Global and Regional Production of Mechanical Woodpulp

	Volume ('000 tons)		Percentage Increase	Percentage Share	
	1954	1964	1954-64	1954	1964
Europe	4, 884	7, 537	54	30. 7	32. 6
U. S. S. R.	730	1, 317	80	4. 6	5. 7
North America	9, 171	11, 867	29	57. 7	51. 3
Latin America	154	403	162	1. 0	1. 7
Africa	3	36	1, 100	-	0. 2
Asia	777	1, 515	95	4. 9	6. 5
Pacific Area	181	457	152	1. 1	2. 0
World Total	15, 900	23, 132	45	100. 0	100. 0

There have also been a number of interesting and significant
developments in the pattern of woodpulp production within some of
the individual regions during the period under consideration.   In
Europe, the main producing nations are of course the three Nordic
countries, Sweden, Norway, and Finland, where large tracks of land
are covered by forests.   Although a few other European woodpulp
producers, such as West Germany and France, have come to the fore

in recent years, the importance of the three Nordic countries has
not diminished.   Instead it has tended to increase quite significantly.
In 1954, Sweden,Norway,and Finland together accounted for 60 per cent
of total European output of all grades of woodpulp, but by 1964 their
combined share of the region's production had shot up to rather more
than 90 per cent.

The most dramatic rate of growth in output among the three
Nordic countries is attributable to Finland.   Production there more
than doubled between 1954 and 1964 to reach a level of nearly 5.9
million tons--representing exactly one quarter of total European
output, compared with a share of rather less than 20 per cent held
by Finland in 1954.   This enormous expansion in pulp production,
and indeed in all the other wood-using sectors, has served to raise
industry's consumption of domestic timber resources in Finland to
well over 30 million solid cubic metres annually, compared with
around 22 million solid cubic metres in 1955.   Understandably, such
a dramatic increase in usage has given rise to some doubts in recent
years about the continuing ability of Finland's forest resources to
sustain a similar rate of growth in future years.   However, the
intensification of existing measures for forest improvement, and
the introduction of a new programme designed to speed up the net
annual growth in the forest's yield, have served to raise Finland's
annual allowable cut to between 50 and 55 million solid cubic metres,
which is as much as two thirds over and above what was in fact used
in 1964.   Furthermore, once the Forestry Finance Committee's
current plans have been fully implemented and the benefits realised,
it will be possible to extract about two and a half times the volume of
timber used at the present time.   As a result, any limitation in
Finland's output of woodpulp in the foreseeable future is likely to be
imposed by demand rather than by supply considerations.

Although Sweden is the most important European producer of
woodpulp, and the third largest producer in the world, its rate of
expansion in recent years has been somewhat below that achieved
by Finland.   Sweden nevertheless raised its output by 3.1 million
tons between 1954 and 1964 (compared with an increase of 3.2
million tons in Finland) to reach a level of 7.1 million tons--rather
more than 30 per cent of aggregate European output of woodpulp.
One of the main features of the Swedish pulp and paper industry in
recent years has been extensive structural rationalisation.   Such
measures are being implemented in order to maintain the industry's
competitiveness with other major producers.   This policy has led
to the closure of old, uneconomic mills, the larger pulp and paper
companies concentrating their production in fewer plants, and a
number of mergers between companies of varying size.

In comparison with the other two Nordic countries, Norway is a relatively small producer of woodpulp. Furthermore, the pace at which it has expanded in recent years has been well below Finland's and Sweden's. Thus between 1954 and 1964, Norwegian production of woodpulp increased by well under 50 per cent (compared with an expansion of 120 per cent in Finland and one of 77 per cent in Sweden) to reach a level just short of 2 million tons. In contrast to Sweden and Finland, although the net annual forest increment is not fully utilised, Norway nevertheless imports a very substantial proportion of its total domestic wood requirements. A large and growing volume of timber has in fact been imported in recent years. The explanation of this somewhat surprising situation is that it may cost more to transport domestic timber to the mill than to import it.

The next largest European woodpulp producers are France and West Germany. Both, of course, are in deficit as far as total woodpulp requirements are concerned, but output in each country, at around 1.5 million tons in 1964, was not very far short of Norway's. France is in fact tending to narrow the gap, since it has recorded the most rapid rate of increase of any of the more important wood-pulp producing countries in Europe. Since 1954 French output has considerably more than doubled. Most of the expansion has taken place in the chemical grades, of which more than 1 million tons were produced in 1964--slightly more than in Norway, which, how-ever, has traditionally placed a much greater proportionate emphasis than other countries on mechanical pulp. Thus in 1964, total Norwegian production of woodpulp was divided almost equally be-tween the chemical and the mechanical grades, while for the rest of Europe as a whole output of chemical pulp exceeded mechanical pulp production by a ratio of above seven to three.

In North America, production of woodpulp has risen much faster in the United States than in Canada in recent years. In 1954, output in the United States amounted to 18.3 million tons, while Canadian production--at 9.7 million tons--was slightly more than half this level. By 1964, however, woodpulp production in the United States had expanded by about 78 per cent to 32.4 million tons, while output by the Canadian industry had advanced at only just over half this rate to reach a total of 13.7 million tons. As a result, Canada's share of total North American production of woodpulp has fallen from around 35 per cent in 1954 to less than 30 per cent in 1964.

A more detailed examination of these aggregate production figures, however, reveals a much heavier concentration on output of the mechanical grades of woodpulp in Canada than in the United

States.   Mechanical pulp accounted for nearly one half of total Canadian woodpulp output in 1964, reflecting the major contribution made by Canada to the world's newsprint requirements.   Canada in fact accounted for around 40 per cent of the global production of news-print in that year, with the bulk being shipped abroad to form over 70 per cent of the world's total exports of this grade.   On the other hand, mechanical pulp represents less than one sixth of total production of woodpulp in the United States.   In the case of both Canada and the United States, however, there has been a trend away from mechanical pulp and towards the chemical grades in recent years, with the latter accounting for a growing share of aggregate output.   This trend has been particularly evident in Canada, where production of mechanical pulp rose by only 21 per cent between 1954 and 1964, whereas chemical pulp output expanded by almost 70 per cent.   Although the difference in rates of growth has been slightly less marked in the United States, the main expansion has nevertheless taken place in the chemical grades.   In volume terms, production of chemical woodpulp increased by as much as 12.6 million tons between 1954 and 1964 to reach a level of 27.2 million tons--representing 45 per cent of total world output.   There has been a particularly rapid growth in output of semi-chemical pulp in the United States, and by the end of this period around 10 per cent of total production of chemical woodpulp consisted of this grade.   Very little semi-chemical pulp, however, is produced in Canada.

The most important producer of woodpulp in Latin America is Brazil, which accounted for well over one half of the region's total output in both 1954 and 1964.   Over this period, Brazil's output has risen from 182,000 to 655,000 tons, and considerable further growth is anticipated during the next few years in view of the country's vast forest resources and the increasing development of fast-growing species.   These factors, together with the government's encourage-ment of the forestry sector by means of fiscal incentives, and the major investments in the Brazilian industry made in recent years by North American and Scandinavian interests, should all tend to combine in stimulating massive development.

The second largest Latin American woodpulp producer is Mexico, where output has trebled between 1954 and 1964 to reach a level of rather more than a quarter of a million tons.   The Mexican government, however, is somewhat concerned that the country's forest resources are not put to optimum use.   It has, therefore, recently introduced a long-term forest control programme, with financial backing from the United Nations.   The successful imple-mentation of this programme should enable the Mexican woodpulp industry to make big strides in coming years; the government's Forestry Agricultural Organisation has in fact already stated that the country's annual timber cut could be raised to 10 million cubic metres within the next fifteen years.

After Brazil and Mexico, Chile is the only other major producer of woodpulp in Latin America--these three countries accounted, in fact, for over 90 per cent of the region's total output in 1964. The rate of expansion achieved by the Chilean industry has been particularly rapid during the period under consideration, since in 1954 output amounted to only a mere 21,000 tons. By 1964, however, production had risen more than eightfold to a level of 174,000 tons, and continued to expand at a very rapid pace in the following two years. Fuller use is being made of the more than 800 million acres of high-quality pine forests in the southern part of the country. In spite of these enormous resources, however, it is possible that the timber supply situation could result in some limitations to the dynamic growth in woodpulp production witnessed in Chile in recent years, unless a substantial volume of planting is initiated.

In Africa, the only two producers of woodpulp in 1954 were South Africa, producing 52,000 tons of chemical pulp, and Swaziland, with an output of 3,000 tons of mechanical pulp. By 1964, a number of other countries--such as Angola, Rhodesia, and Morocco--had developed small-scale production facilities, but South Africa and Swaziland nevertheless accounted for as much as 84 per cent of the region's total production of 385,000 tons of woodpulp. South Africa's share in this total amounted to 225,000 tons, while Swaziland's single woodpulp mill recorded a production level of 97,000 tons.

Asian production of woodpulp is dominated by Japan, which accounted for just over three quarters of the region's total output in 1964. The relative importance of Japan was in fact somewhat greater in 1954, but since that time small local industries have been established and developed in a number of Asian countries, and Japan's very considerable rate of growth has not been sufficient to prevent it from losing ground slightly within the region as a whole. Japanese output of woodpulp has nevertheless more than trebled between 1954 and 1964 to reach a level of over 5 million tons, divided approximately in the ratio of 4 to 1 in favour of chemical pulp. The country's domestic timber resources, however, have been insufficient to sustain this very sharp expansion, and Japan has found it necessary to import large and increasing quantities of pulpwood and chips in recent years.

In the Pacific Area, the last of the seven geographical regions into which the world is divided for the purposes of this study, production of woodpulp is confined to two countries--Australia and New Zealand.   One of the most interesting features revealed by a closer examination of production trends in this region is the dramatic rise in the relative importance of New Zealand.   In 1954, the Pacific Area's woodpulp production amounted to 335,000 tons, of which Australia accounted for just over three quarters and New Zealand for almost one quarter.   By 1964 the region's output had increased by over 170 per cent to 914,000 tons, which was almost equally divided between the two countries.   Thus, while Australian production had rather less than doubled over this decade, New Zealand's had expanded more than fivefold to reach a level of 444,000 tons. Another interesting feature of the Pacific Area's performance in 1964 is that in both Australia and New Zealand, and accordingly in the region as a whole, output was almost equally divided between the mechanical and chemical grades of woodpulp.

In general, therefore, the 1954-64 decade has witnessed a very significant expansion in the woodpulp industry of each of the seven main geographical regions and in all of the major producing countries, with a particularly rapid growth in production of semi-chemical and high yield chemical pulp being noticeable in recent years.   While the fastest rate of increase has been achieved by the less industrialised and smallest producing regions, where production facilities tend to be limited to a small number of rapidly developing countries, the vast bulk of the tonnage expansion in output over this period has been accounted for by the two major producing regions--North America and Europe.   Thus, of the aggregate increase in world woodpulp production of around 29.5 million tons between 1954 and 1964, the North American and European industries recorded a joint expansion of no less than 21 million tons.   The regional pattern of the world pulp industry has therefore tended to become even more unevenly distributed, and in view of the relative pace of development in the main producing centres, this trend is likely to continue during the foreseeable future.   The extent to which this concentration of output in the northern hemisphere is offset by an expanding volume of trade between the more important and the less important producing regions is a subject which is examined in the following chapter.

CHAPTER **3** THE
SIGNIFICANCE OF
INTERNATIONAL TRADE

During the 1954-64 period there has been a very substantial
expansion in the volume of world trade in woodpulp. The growth
in international trade has in fact proceeded at a faster pace than the
level of woodpulp production, with the result that a growing proportion of output has been moving into international trade. Thus in
1957, world exports of woodpulp represented around 15.4 per cent
of the volume of output, with the proportion rising progressively to
15.9 per cent in 1961, 16.2 per cent in 1963,and 16.5 per cent in
1964. In general, the faster growth in trade reflects three
influences: an increasing deficiency of woodpulp, in volume terms,
among the relatively low consumption regions; a growing exportable
surplus in some of the high consumption regions; and a tendency
towards regional specialisation in the production of certain grades
of woodpulp.

This trend towards a growing proportion of the world's woodpulp output entering into international trade contrasts with the
performance in the paper and paperboard sector. There, world
exports as a proportion of global production fell from 17.5 per
cent in 1954 to 16.7 per cent in 1964. As, from a national point
of view, exporting a more highly processed product than an industrial raw material is more desirable, one might have expected the
reverse of this trend. Of course, the opposite preference is held
by importing countries, and this is generally expressed in the form
of low tariffs (or none at all) on woodpulp, and relatively high
protectionist duties on paper and paperboard. The tariff structure
has clearly been the major determinant of the relative trends in
trade in pulp and paper. Not only this: At the same time it has
tended to retard or discourage the degree of vertical integration
within the pulp and paper industries of some of the major countries
which have timber resources surplus to their own domestic requirements.

Not surprisingly, most of the world's exports of woodpulp are
supplied by the two principal producing regions--Europe and North
America--whose dominating position has changed little in recent

years.   In 1954 these two regions accounted for a combined share
of over 98 per cent of aggregate world exports of woodpulp, and in
1964 their share was still as high as 95 per cent.

Although European exports are still half as large again as North
America's, the latter have been growing at an appreciably faster
rate.   As a result, North America has raised its share of global
woodpulp exports from less than 35 per cent in 1954 to 38 per cent
in 1964, while Europe's share has fallen from 63.5 to just over 57
per cent during the same period.   Nevertheless, a very much
larger proportion of European output of woodpulp moves across
national frontiers--as much as one third in 1964, compared with
little more than 11 per cent in the case of North America.

TABLE 21

Global and Regional Exports of Woodpulp

	Volume ('000 tons)		Percentage Increase	Percentage Share	
	1954	1964	1954-64	1954	1964
Europe	4,814	7,839	63	63.5	57.1
U.S.S.R.	114	291	155	1.5	2.1
North America	2,623	5,215	99	34.6	38.0
Latin America	6	28	367	0.1	0.2
Africa	–	289	–	–	2.1
Asia	–	–	–	–	–
Pacific Area	22	74	236	0.3	0.5
World Total	7,579	13,736	81	100.0	100.0

One of the most interesting facts revealed by the above table
is the very appreciable increase which has taken place in African
exports of woodpulp in recent years.   No woodpulp was exported
in 1954, but ten years later exports from Africa (mainly accounted
for by South Africa and Swaziland) had shot up to 289,000 tons, and
were virtually equal to the level of exports achieved by Russia.
The U.S.S.R. has nevertheless effected a large increase in exports
over this decade--one in excess of 150 per cent in fact--yet it still
accounts for only just over 2 per cent of aggregate world exports of
woodpulp.   Thanks to the very rapid development of the country's
pulping facilities, however, and the gradual harnessing of the
enormous forest resources of the eastern region of Siberia, there
is little doubt that Russia will become an increasingly significant
force in the international woodpulp market in coming years.

Elsewhere, the Pacific Area has been successful in more than trebling its volume of woodpulp exports to 74,000 tons during the 1954-64 period, although its share of world exports has risen to only one half of one per cent. Latin American exports were little more than one third of this level in 1964, while the Asian region has not featured as a woodpulp exporter.

A consideration of the corresponding statistics in respect of regional imports of woodpulp reveals that a very large proportion of the volume of world trade in woodpulp is of an intra-regional rather than an inter-regional nature. In 1964, for example, Europe and North America accounted for a combined share of 95.1 per cent of world exports of woodpulp, and 85.5 per cent of aggregate imports (although even higher proportions in 1954--98.1 per cent and 88.1 per cent, respectively). There is of course a considerable volume of exports from North America to Europe and from Europe to the United States. Yet much of aggregate world trade in woodpulp takes the form, on the one hand, of shipments from the Nordic countries to the U.K. and Continental Europe, and, on the other hand, of exports from Canada to the U.S.A.

TABLE 22

Global and Regional Imports of Woodpulp

	Volume ('000 tons)		Percentage Increase	Percentage Share	
	1954	1964	1954-64	1954	1964
Europe	4,536	8,607	90	60.2	63.3
U.S.S.R.	41	136	232	0.5	1.0
North America	2,103	3,016	43	27.9	22.2
Latin America	549	517	-6	7.3	3.8
Africa	30	104	247	0.4	0.8
Asia	189	963	410	2.5	7.1
Pacific Area	86	245	185	1.2	1.8
World Total	7,534	13,588	80	100.0	100.0

The above table illustrates the outstanding position of Europe, which has tended to become an even more important market for imported woodpulp in recent years, accounting in 1964 for little short of two thirds of total world imports. On the other hand, the relative significance of the much smaller North American market has diminished somewhat, with imports in 1964 being little more than one third of the volume of European imports. Of the remaining

geographical regions, the most important as a user of imported
woodpulp is Asia, with imports having risen from 189,000 tons in
1954 to little short of a million tons in 1964.   Latin American woodpulp imports, however, were about 6 per cent lower in 1964 than in
1954, reflecting the much greater degree of self-sufficiency which
has been attained.   Many new pulp mills have been set up, primarily
in such countries as Brazil, Mexico, and Chile, and regional production has risen steeply.   Imports into the Pacific Area have
nearly trebled since 1954, while even larger proportionate in-
creases--although lower in tonnage terms--have occurred in both
Africa and the U.S.S.R.

A comparison of the export and import statistics set out in
Tables 21 and 22 is presented below, indicating the extent to which
the various geographical regions are net exporters or net importers
of woodpulp.

TABLE 23

Net Regional Trade in Woodpulp ('000 tons)

	1954	1959	1964
Europe	+278	+ 86	- 768
U.S.S.R.	+ 73	+153	+ 155
North America	+520	+604	+2,199
Latin America	-543	-482	- 489
Africa	- 30	+ 22	+ 185
Asia	-189	-278	- 963
Pacific	- 64	- 63	- 171

Note: A plus sign indicates that the region is a net
       exporter, while a minus sign denotes a net
       importing region.   Due to the leads and lags of
       international trade, however, the total figures of
       net imports and net exports in each column do not
       balance precisely.

A number of interesting trends are revealed by the above
presentation of net regional trade in woodpulp.   On the one hand,
although North America's imports have risen quite substantially in
recent years, a much faster and greater absolute increase in
exports has resulted in the achievement of a progressively larger
trading surplus.   Since 1954, in fact, North America has more
than quadrupled its net exports of woodpulp to a level of 2.2 million
tons in 1964, with most of the expansion taking place in the last five
years.   In so doing, it has raised its share of aggregate regional

net exports from rather less than 60 per cent in 1954 to over 86 per cent ten years later.   On the other hand, Europe, the second largest regional producer of woodpulp, so far from being the not insignificant net exporter it was in 1954--when it accounted for nearly one third of total regional net exports--is running up a steadily growing deficit.   By 1964, in fact, net imports into Europe had risen to over three quarters of a million tons, representing a similar proportion of around one third of the aggregate net inter-regional flow of woodpulp.

Apart from North America, the only other region which has consistently achieved a net exporting position over the past decade is the U.S.S.R.   Although the extent of the export surplus has shown little signs of growth during the past few years, between 1954 and 1964 as a whole the volume of net exports was,in fact,doubled. Africa has also swung into a surplus during the course of the decade under consideration, and by 1964 the level of net exports, at 185,000 tons, exceeded that achieved by the U.S.S.R.

Another interesting fact which may be deduced from Table 23 is the very significant expansion in net regional trade in recent years.   As noted earlier in this chapter, a large proportion of the total volume of international trade in woodpulp represents move-ments between countries within a particular region.   Such move-ments cover exports from Canada to the U.S.A., and from the Nordic countries to the U.K. and the Continental European countries. A consideration of the net regional export figures in Table 23 (which equal net regional imports apart from a slight incidence of leads and lags in international trade movements) reveals that the total volume of net regional trade in woodpulp remained broadly un-changed between 1954 and 1959, but during the following five years very nearly trebled to reach a level of 2.5 million tons.   This compares with an expansion in exports as a whole between 1954 and 1964 of 81 per cent, and implies that a growing proportion of inter-national trade in woodpulp is of an inter-regional nature, although the volume is still dwarfed by the larger element of intra-regional trade.

International trade in woodpulp is very heavily weighted in favour of the chemical grades, with mechanical woodpulp accounting for a disproportionately small share of aggregate exports.   Thus in 1964, chemical woodpulp accounted for over 88 per cent of the total volume of woodpulp exports of 13.7 million tons--about 5 per cent more than the share held ten years earlier.   Looked at in another way, just over one fifth of world production of chemical woodpulp

TABLE 24

Global and Regional Exports of Chemical and Mechanical Woodpulp in 1964

	Chemical Woodpulp			Mechanical Woodpulp		
	Exports ('000 tons)	Percentage Share	Exports as a Percentage of Production	Exports ('000 tons)	Percentage Share	Exports as a Percentage of Production
Europe	6,570	54.0	41.3	1,269	81.1	16.8
U.S.S.R.	289	2.4	8.9	2	0.1	0.2
North America	4,926	40.4	14.4	289	18.5	2.4
Latin America	24	0.2	3.0	4	0.3	1.0
Africa	289	2.4	82.8	–	–	–
Asia	–	–	–	–	–	–
Pacific Area	74	0.6	76.2	–	–	–
World Total	12,172	100.0	20.2	1,564	100.0	6.8

found its way into international trade in 1964, while exports of
mechanical woodpulp represented less than 7 per cent of global output of this grade.   Exports of mechanical pulp are relatively small
because it is largely the raw material for newsprint, where economies of scale favour large, integrated operations and exports of the
end product.   On the other hand, the numerous grades and qualities
of chemical woodpulp, together with a certain element of regional
specialisation in production, tend to make for a much larger volume
of two-way trade both between individual countries within a particular
region and between the various geographical regions under consideration.

In mechanical pulp, Europe accounts for well over 80 per cent
of world exports, with North America contributing much of the rest.
The predominance of Europe in mechanical pulp trade is in part
attributable to the gearing of the Norwegian industry to production
and export of this grade.   The pattern of exports is rather more
balanced in the case of the chemical grades, however, with Europe
accounting for 54 per cent of the total in 1964 and North America for
slightly more than 40 per cent.   Among the remaining regions, both
the U.S.S.R. and Africa made a small but significant contribution to
global exports of chemical woodpulp in 1964--each accounting for
2.4 per cent of the total--whereas in the case of mechanical woodpulp all but a mere 6,000 tons of global exports emanated either
from Europe or North America.

In addition to accounting for a considerably larger share of
global exports of both chemical and mechanical woodpulp than North
America, the importance of Europe is further highlighted by the
large contribution it makes to international trade.   The proportion
of European output moving into exports amounted to as much as 41
per cent in 1964 for chemical woodpulp--compared with less than
15 per cent in the case of North America.   By contrast, nearly 17
per cent of European mechanical pulp was exported as against only
2.4 per cent of North America's output.   Elsewhere, a very high
proportion of output of chemical woodpulp is exported by Africa
(nearly 83 per cent) and the Pacific Area (over 76 per cent), although
the actual quantities involved are not particularly large within the
context of the total flow of trade in woodpulp.

The corresponding pattern of global and regional imports of
chemical and mechanical woodpulp in 1964 is set out in Table 25.
From these statistics it can be seen that the two principal consuming
regions--North America and Europe--account for a significantly
larger share of world imports of mechanical than of chemical pulp,

TABLE 25

Global and Regional Imports of Chemical and Mechanical Woodpulp in 1964

	Chemical Woodpulp			Mechanical Woodpulp		
	Imports ('000 tons)	Percentage Share	Imports as a Percentage of Consumption	Imports ('000 tons)	Percentage Share	Imports as a Percentage of Consumption
Europe	7,328	61.8	43.7	1,279	74.2	16.9
U.S.S.R.	136	1.1	4.4	-	-	-
North America	2,668	22.5	8.3	348	20.2	2.8
Latin America	470	4.0	37.8	47	2.7	10.5
Africa	100	0.9	62.5	4	0.2	10.0
Asia	928	7.7	15.4	35	2.1	2.3
Pacific Area	234	2.0	37.9	11	0.6	2.4
World Total	11,864	100.0	19.8	1,724	100.0	7.4

Note: Due to the leads and lags of international trade, the global import figures set out above do not precisely match the corresponding export figures shown in Table 24.

although in both sectors they occupy a dominant position.   Thus in
1964, North America and Europe accounted for a combined share of
over 94 per cent of global imports of mechanical woodpulp, although
their share of chemical woodpulp imports was some 10 per cent less
than this.

Table 25 brings out the point that mechanical pulp does not
feature prominently in international trade compared with chemical
woodpulp, where the relationship between the volume of production
and trade is much more weighted in favour of trade.   Of all the
regions, Europe is in fact the most heavily dependent on imports of
mechanical pulp, both in volume and in proportionate terms, since
imports represent almost 17 per cent of total consumption.   Latin
America and Africa each rely on imports for around 10 per cent of
their requirements, the U. S. S. R. imports none at all, while imports
into North America, Asia,and the Pacific Area represent only between
2 and 3 per cent of each region's total usage of mechanical woodpulp.

On the other hand, the much greater significance of international
trade in chemical woodpulp is reflected in the fact that an average of
around 20 per cent of regional consumption is based on imported
supplies.   Three regions--the U. S. S. R. , Asia, and North America--
have a below-average dependence on imports, although in absolute
terms the North American region nevertheless represents a major
market for chemical woodpulp. since it accounted for well over one
fifth of global imports in 1964.   In proportionate terms, the African
region was the most heavily dependent on imports in 1964, with
imports forming nearly two thirds of consumption, while Latin
America and the Pacific Area each imported well over one third of
their total requirements.   As in the case of mechanical woodpulp,
however, the most important market for imported chemical woodpulp is the European region, which accounted for nearly two thirds
of global imports, which in turn represented well over two fifths of
aggregate consumption in Europe in 1964.

Passing now to a brief consideration of the relative importance
of some of the major countries within each of the geographical
regions, it is interesting to note that, in Europe, the three Nordic
countries together accounted for rather less than two thirds of the
aggregate regional output of all grades of woodpulp in 1964.   Their
combined share of total European exports, however, was well in
excess of 90 per cent.   In spite of a generally rising volume of
exports from such countries as Portugal, Yugoslavia, West Germany,
and Austria, the three Nordic countries have been successful in

maintaining their overwhelming position in European woodpulp exports, as a similar share was held in 1954.   Obviously Scandinavian forest resources are far from being denuded.

Sweden is by far the largest exporter among the three Nordic countries.   In 1964 it accounted for almost one half of total European woodpulp exports of 7.8 million tons.   Its share has tended to decline slightly during the decade under consideration, however, owing to the much more rapid growth in exports achieved by Finland.   Thus, while Swedish exports of woodpulp increased by 56 per cent between 1954 and 1964 to reach a level of 3.8 million tons, Finnish exports expanded at a rate half as fast again.   In achieving an expansion of this magnitude, Finland has been able to raise its share of European woodpulp exports from about 26 per cent to almost 30 per cent over the 1954-64 period.   One particularly striking feature of Finland's export performance should be pointed out: Exports of mechanical pulp were in fact slightly lower in 1964 than ten years earlier.   All of the expansion has accordingly taken place in exports of the chemical grades, which more than doubled over this period to reach a level of nearly 2.2 million tons.   This represents just under one third of total European exports of chemical woodpulp in 1964.   So Finland is following the normal course of highly organised and efficient industry by switching production resources increasingly into more highly processed products.

The relative importance of Norway as an exporter has tended to decline in recent years.   The country's exportable surplus has risen by only 220,000 tons, or by less than 30 per cent, during the 1954-64 period.   At the same time, total European exports have grown by 3 million tons, representing an increase of 63 per cent. There is one notable feature of the Norwegian woodpulp trade: Although the country's total exports were only one quarter the size of those of Sweden in 1964, its exports of mechanical woodpulp were considerably in excess of Sweden's.   Hence, while its exports of chemical woodpulp represented less than 6 per cent of the European total in 1964, Norway accounted for very nearly one half of the region's aggregate exports of mechanical woodpulp in that year.

In the import sector, the U.K. represents Europe's, and indeed the world's, largest market.   In 1964, 3.3 million tons of woodpulp were imported into the U.K.--little short of two· fifths of Europe's total imports, and nearly a quarter of global imports. Both inside and outside Europe, however, the needs of other countries have risen more rapidly than those of the U.K.   In 1954 the U.K. held an even more important position, accounting for almost

half of Europe's aggregate imports and over 28 per cent of the
world's total imports of woodpulp.   Although the United States
imported slightly more chemical woodpulp than the U.K. in 1964
the latter is by far the largest market for imported mechanical
woodpulp.   By and large it absorbs half the world's total imports.
The explanation is simple enough.   Britain has a large newsprint
industry of its own to ensure that the freedom of the press is not
imperiled by the vicissitudes of foreign supplies, but it lacks the
raw material to keep the newsprint mills going.

Although the U.K. is striving to develop its indigenous forest
resources, and has recently seen the establishment of two or three
fully-integrated mills, domestic supplies of papermaking species of
timber remain scarce.   Less than 8 per cent of the U.K. is under
forest, a smaller proportion than any other European country with
the exception of Ireland and the Netherlands.   Thus, even though an
increasing share of the U.K.'s paper and paperboard requirements
is being supplied by foreign mills, there is little doubt that it will
remain the largest single market for imported woodpulp in the foreseeable future.

After the U.K., the next largest European importers of woodpulp are West Germany, France,and Italy, although the combined
volume of imports into these three countries in 1964 was slightly
less than that entering the U.K.   West Germany, France,and Italy,
however, have a greater proportionate dependence on foreign
supplies of chemical woodpulp than the U.K. (because the latter
imports relatively more paper).   Their aggregate imports of
mechanical woodpulp, on the other hand, are little more than one
quarter of the size of the U.K.'s import requirements.

One significant fact revealed by a consideration of these three
countries' individual performance is that while France was easily
the largest importer in 1954, West Germany had assumed that
position by 1964 due to the much more rapid growth in the needs of
its paper industry.

In North America, the major exporter of woodpulp is of course
Canada, but the United States has been gaining considerably in
importance as an exporter in recent years.   Between 1954 and 1964
exports of woodpulp from the United States more than trebled to
reach a level of nearly 1.6 million tons, equal to just over 30 per
cent of total North American exports.   Some ten years earlier the
United States' share was less than 17 per cent.   On the import side,
the United States accounts for the bulk of North American woodpulp
imports.   Canada is, of course, a large exporter and imports only

very small quantities of speciality pulp.   It is interesting to note, however, that the United States has reduced its dependence on net imports of woodpulp quite appreciably in recent years.   Thus, while imports rose by 900, 000 tons between 1954 and 1964 to reach a level of 2.9 million tons, an increase of over 1.1 million tons was achieved in exports.   As a result, the volume of net imports into the United States over this period fell from 1.6 million tons to less than 1.4 million tons.

Latin America's dependence on imported woodpulp has lessened slightly in recent years, largely due to the much greater degree of self-sufficiency achieved by Brazil.   In 1954, Brazil imported around 200, 000 tons of chemical woodpulp, representing well over one· third of the Latin American region's total imports.   By 1964, however, imports into Brazil had fallen to 31, 000 tons--just 6 per cent of total Latin American woodpulp imports.   The largest importer in this region is now Argentina, followed by Mexico and Colombia.   In general, however, imports have been kept down partly by the rapid development of Latin America's indigenous forest resources and partly by import curbs necessitated by foreign currency shortage.   Although the region's woodpulp exports amounted to only 28, 000 tons in 1964--of which nearly half was accounted for by Chile--considerable expansion has taken place in subsequent years.   By the end of the present decade Chile, further- more, is planning to produce an exportable woodpulp surplus of the order of 400, 000 tons a year.

Although the African region did not export any woodpulp at all in 1954, exports had reached a level of 289, 000 tons ten years later. The bulk of this was accounted for by South Africa (138, 000 tons) and Swaziland (99, 000 tons), but Morocco has also built up a sizable export trade and in fact exports a substantial proportion of its wood- pulp production.   In 1964 Africa exported nearly three times as much woodpulp as it imported, the principal importer, accounting for over half the regional total, being the United Arab Republic.

Japan is the principal importer in the Asian region and in 1964 imported nearly 600, 000 tons of woodpulp--about 60 per cent of total imports into the region.   Japan's imports of woodpulp have risen sharply in recent years.   When account is also taken of the growing volume of imports of pulpwood and chips, it is apparent that Japan's indigenous timber resources are supplying a diminishing proportion of the country's rapidly expanding requirements.

Finally, in the Pacific Area, New Zealand accounted for all of the region's woodpulp exports, which increased from 22,000 tons in 1954 to 74,000 tons in 1964. On the other hand, Australian imports, which over this period have risen quite sharply from 80,000 to 223,000 tons, form the bulk of the region's total requirements.

This chapter has been concerned with presenting a broad assessment of trends in international and inter-regional trade in woodpulp, following an examination of the main developments which have taken place in woodpulp production during the 1954-64 period. As a sequence to this analysis, the next chapter moves on to a consideration of regional trends in consumption during this decade, and a more detailed analysis of the regional pattern of supply and demand in respect of woodpulp, pulpwood, and paper and paper-board.

4

THE REGIONAL
PATTERN OF
SUPPLY AND DEMAND

If the relatively small fluctuations which take place in the level of stocks between the end of one year and the next are ignored, world consumption of woodpulp can be equated with the volume of output in any given year. Thus, returning to the production figures quoted in Chapter 2, global consumption of woodpulp, which amounted to 46.7 million tons in 1954, had risen by 79 per cent to reach a level of 83.4 million tons by 1964.

The regional pattern of woodpulp usage, on the other hand, clearly cannot be equated with the regional level of production, in view of the existence of fairly substantial inter-regional flows. If international trade is taken into account, however, the regional pattern of woodpulp consumption in 1964 was along the lines set out in Table 26. (In this context, it should be noted that consumption of woodpulp is taken to mean woodpulp which is used to manufacture paper and paperboard in the geographical region in question, irrespective of whether the final product is exported outside the region.)

As far as regional usage of woodpulp is concerned--or the actual conversion of woodpulp into paper and paperboard in particular regions, as distinct from regional consumption of the finished product--the following table reveals that North America, with only 6.4 per cent of the world's population, accounted for rather more than half (52.8 per cent) of global consumption of woodpulp in 1964. Rather less disproportionately, Europe's share of total woodpulp consumption was rather more than twice as large as its share of the world population. A similar ratio is found in the case of the Pacific Area, but for all of the remaining regions a considerably less than unitary relationship exists between their share of woodpulp usage and world population. At the extreme, Asia, with well over half of the world's population, accounted for only just over 9 per cent of aggregate consumption, while Africa's share was a mere 0.2 per cent in 1964, yet this region contains over 9 per cent of the world's population.

TABLE 26

Global and Regional Consumption of Woodpulp in 1964 ('000 tons)

	Production	Imports	Exports	Consumption	Percentage Share of Consumption	Percentage Share of Population
Europe	23,548	8,607	7,839	24,316	29.2	13.4
U.S.S.R.	4,551	136	291	4,396	4.3	7.0
North America	46,172	3,016	5,215	43,973	52.8	6.4
Latin America	1,198	517	28	1,687	2.1	7.1
Africa	385	104	289	200	0.2	9.3
Asia	6,623	963	–	7,586	9.1	56.3
Pacific Area	914	245	74	1,085	1.3	0.5
World Total	83,391	13,588	13,736	83,243	100.0	100.0

Note: Due to the leads and lags of international trade, the global volume of exports recorded in 1964 exceeds recorded imports. Since world consumption is calculated on the basis of production, plus imports, less exports, the global consumption figure in the above table is slightly lower than that of world production.

These striking regional disparities in per capita usage of wood-pulp are not lessened to any significant extent even if net regional trade flows of paper and paperboard are taken into account.   From the statistics set out in Table 27 below, it can be seen that total net exports from those regions enjoying a positive relationship between their proportion of world woodpulp usage and their share of world population (i.e. North America, Europe, and the Pacific Area) amounted to only 2.8 million tons in 1964, which represented a mere 3.3 per cent of global consumption of woodpulp.   Nevertheless, this volume of net imports of paper and paperboard into the regions where usage is lowest (Asia, Africa and Latin America) served to augment their combined level of consumption by nearly 30 per cent.

TABLE 27

Net Regional Trade in Woodpulp and Paper
and Paperboard in 1964

	Net Trade in Woodpulp ('000 tons)	Net Imports as a Proportion of Woodpulp Consumption (per cent)	Net Exports as a Proportion of Woodpulp Production (per cent)	Net Trade in Paper and Paperboard ('000 tons)
Europe	- 768	3.2	-	+ 712
U.S.S.R.	+ 155	-	3.4	+ 3
North America	+2,199	-	4.8	+2,373
Latin America	- 489	29.0	-	-1,037
Africa	+ 185	-	48.1	- 538
Asia	- 963	12.7	-	- 902
Pacific Area	- 171	15.8	-	- 325

Note: A plus sign denotes net exports, and a minus sign net imports.
       Due to the leads and lags of international trade, which
       normally result in a higher level of exports than imports
       being recorded in any given year, the figures in the first and
       final columns of the above table do not cancel out precisely.

Another point of interest which emerges from the above table is the relative dependence of the deficit regions on net imports.   In spite of the fairly substantial volume of net imports into Europe in 1964, these represented only just over 3 per cent of the region's

total woodpulp usage.   In the remaining deficit regions there was a
very much heavier proportionate reliance on imported supplies in
1964--ranging from nearly 13 per cent in Asia to as much as 29 per
cent in the case of Latin America.   Looking at the opposite side of
the picture, North American net exports represented less than 5
per cent of the region's total production of woodpulp in 1964.
Russia encourages woodpulp exports and discourages the use of
paper, which is low enough by Western standards, with the result
that exports in 1964 accounted for more than 3 per cent of woodpulp
output.   In the case of Africa, it is surprising to find that nearly
half the region's output found its way into net exports in 1964.   This
reflects,however, the establishment of pulp mills, geared to exporting, in South Africa, Swaziland, and Morocco.   In view of the early
stage of economic development through which most of the remaining
areas of the continent are passing, woodpulp requirements are still
of a relatively limited nature.

Before turning to a consideration of the prospective regional
pattern of demand for woodpulp in coming years, and the implications for production and trade in the future, it may be interesting
to measure in broad terms the extent to which the main deficit
regions--Latin America, Africa, Asia,and the Pacific Area--are
currently dependent on a net imported supply of both woodpulp and
paper and paperboard.   An attempt to do this in respect of 1964 is
made in Table 28.   Having set out details of paper and paperboard
output, net trade,and consumption, this table shows, first, the
significance of net imports as a proportion of consumption, and then
indicates the extent to which regional production of paper is based
on net imports of woodpulp.   The sum of these two figures, which is
shown in the final column of the table, accordingly represents the
proportion of paper consumption in each region which is based on net
imports of either woodpulp or paper and paperboard.

From such an analysis it can be seen that Latin America is
dependent on net imported supplies of either woodpulp or paper and
paperboard for as much as 42.5 per cent of its total consumption of
the latter.   The Pacific Area's reliance on net imports is equivalent
to rather more than one third of its total consumption, but Asia's
imbalance is much less marked, with only 13 per cent of paper
consumption being based on net imported supplies.   The African
region is a relatively large net importer of paper and paperboard.
On the other hand, it enjoys a net surplus in woodpulp exports.   In
view of this, the paper equivalent of net woodpulp exports--expressed
as a percentage of paper and paperboard consumption--must be
deducted from the calculation of net imports of paper as a percentage

TABLE 28

The Extent of the Deficit Regions' Dependence on Net Imports
of Woodpulp and Paper and Paperboard in 1964

Paper and Paperboard

	Production ('000 tons)	Net Imports ('000 tons)	Consumption ('000 tons)	Proportion of Consumption Supplied by Net Imports (per cent)	Proportion of Consumption Based on Net Imports of Woodpulp* (per cent)	Proportion of Consumption Based on Net Imports of Woodpulp or Paper and Paperboard (per cent)
Latin America	2,476	1,037	3,513	29.5	13.0	42.5
Africa	722	538	1,260	42.7	+12.6**	30.1
Asia	12,879	902	13,781	6.5	6.5	13.0
Pacific Area	1,074	325	1,399	23.2	11.4	34.6

Note: * Calculated on the basis of an average of 1.07 tons of pulp equalling one ton of paper and paperboard.

** Africa is a net exporter of woodpulp, and hence this offsets to some extent the over-all significance of net imports of paper and paperboard.

of consumption. Once this correction is made, the proportion of
paper and paperboard consumption based on net imported supplies
comes out at just over 30 per cent.

It is also worthy of note that, as far as woodpulp is concerned,
only one of the four deficit regions--Latin America--has achieved
a faster rate of growth in production than in consumption during the
1954-64 period. Hence, unlike Europe, Asia,and the Pacific Area,
Latin America's proportionate dependence on supplies of woodpulp
imported from outside the region has been reduced. In the other
three regions, however, import requirements have risen both in
absolute and in proportionate terms.

North America and the U.S.S.R. each have a net exportable
surplus of both pulp and paper. On the other hand, Europe, while
being a net exporter of paper and paperboard, has now become a
net importer of woodpulp. The magnitude of net exports of paper
and net imports of woodpulp, however, were broadly comparable
in 1964, and hence at that time Europe was neither a deficit nor a
surplus region, but was nicely balanced at a state of over-all self-
sufficiency as far as these two products are concerned.

Most of the relatively limited net trade in fibreboard is between
Europe and North America, and therefore the inclusion of this
product has comparatively little effect on the over-all dependence of
the deficit regions on outside supplies of woodpulp and pulp-based
products. There is, however, one additional factor which, in
certain instances, has a significant bearing on the above calculations
of net regional deficits and surpluses--the existence of a fairly substantial volume of international trade in pulpwood. Between 1954
and 1964 world exports of pulpwood increased by almost one third,
rising from just under 10 million cubic metres to a level of 13.2
million cubic metres. It is perhaps significant, however, that the
pace of expansion in the pulpwood trade has been very considerably
slower than that in international trade in woodpulp--which rose by 81
per cent over this same period. This may be largely taken as
reflecting the preference of producing countries in general to export
products such as woodpulp or paper and paperboard, which have a
much larger element of added value than pulpwood.

In order to make a comparison of the relative significance of the
international movement of pulpwood, it might not be unreasonable to
assume for the purposes of this analysis that it is transformed into
either chemical or mechanical pulp in approximately the same proportions as world production of woodpulp in 1964 . This was, broadly

speaking, in a ratio of three to one in favour of the chemical grades.
Thus, using an average conversion factor of four cubic metres of
pulpwood to one ton of woodpulp, it may be calculated that the
volume of international trade in pulpwood in 1964 represented something of the order of 3.3 million tons of woodpulp--little short of one
quarter of the actual volume of trade in woodpulp in that year.

Details of the regional pattern of trade are set out in the
following table:

TABLE 29

Global and Regional Trade in Pulpwood ('000 cubic metres)

	Exports		Imports		Net Trade	
	1954	1964	1954	1964	1954	1964
Europe	4,110	5,579	4,162	9,998	- 52	-4,419
U.S.S.R.	2	4,046	279	-	-277	+4,046
North America	5,846	3,140	5,129	1,845	+717	+1,295
Latin America	-	409	-	-	-	+ 409
Africa	-	4	-	1	-	+ 3
Asia	-	21	89	679	- 89	- 658
Pacific Area	-	-	-	-	-	-
World Total	9,958	13,199	9,659	12,523	+299	+ 676

Note: A plus sign denotes a net exporter, and a minus sign a net
importer. As recorded exports were higher than recorded
imports in each of the years considered in the above table--
largely reflecting the leads and lags of international trade--
a positive balance is shown under aggregate regional net
trade.

A number of interesting facts are revealed by this table. Looking first at the export side, world exports of pulpwood in 1954 were
accounted for almost exclusively by North America and Europe.
However, by 1964, European exports had been raised quite sub-
stantially--by nearly 1.5 million cubic metres, or by over one third--
whereas exports from North America had fallen by almost 50
per cent, reflecting the growing demands of the domestic pulp and
paper industry. The combined exports of these two regions were in
fact lower in 1964 than ten years earlier, but this decline was considerably more than offset by a dramatic upsurge in Russian exports
of pulpwood. These rose from a mere 2,000 cubic metres in 1954
to over 4 million cubic metres in 1964, equal to 30 per cent of world

exports. This astronomical increase follows the rapid development of the Russian forestry industry, but it may be assumed that
in the years to come policy will veer towards raising exports of
woodpulp, possibly at the expense of pulpwood shipments. A
large number of woodpulp mills are under construction or at the
planning stage in Russia and as they come on stream the exportable
surplus of woodpulp will tend to grow. Elsewhere, both Africa and
Asia made small contributions to world exports of pulpwood in 1964,
while Latin American exports rose during the decade under consideration to a level of over 400,000 cubic metres.

North America and Europe were the major pulpwood importers
in 1954, but by 1964 North America's import requirements had
fallen by nearly two thirds, while European imports had risen by
5.8 million cubic metres to the point where they represented about
80 per cent of global imports of pulpwood. Although relatively
insignificant in comparison with the volume of European imports,
there has nevertheless been a noticeable upsurge in Asian imports
of pulpwood during the 1954-64 period, accounted for in the main
by Japan's rapidly growing requirements.

In net terms, the principal deficit regions for pulpwood are
Europe and, to a lesser extent, Asia, while the major net exporting
regions are the U.S.S.R., North America, and Latin America. One
final feature of interest in this table is that, over the period in
question, aggregate net regional trade has grown much more rapidly
than international trade in pulpwood as a whole. This indicates that
an increasing proportion of international trade is of an inter-regional,
as opposed to an intra-regional nature. In 1954, total net regional
exports of pulpwood amounted to 717,000 cubic metres--equivalent
to around 7 per cent of total pulpwood exports. By 1964, however,
aggregate net regional exports, at 5.8 million cubic metres, represented nearly 44 per cent of global exports.

With regard to the four deficit regions considered in Table 28,
the inclusion of net trade in pulpwood in the over-all analysis does
not have a particularly significant effect on the calculations that have
already been made. Thus, using the conversion factor of four cubic
metres of pulpwood to one ton of woodpulp, and 1.07 tons of woodpulp
to 1 ton of paper or paperboard, the proportion of each of these
region's total consumption of paper and paperboard which was based
on net imports of paper, woodpulp, or pulpwood was as follows in
1964:

	Per Cent
Latin America	39.8
Africa	30.0
Asia	14.1
Pacific Area	34.6

The inclusion of pulpwood, however, has a much more marked effect on the European picture. It will be recalled that the volume of Europe's net exports of paper in 1964 was almost exactly the same as its net imports of woodpulp. Hence in terms of inter-regional trade in these two products Europe was in balance--in other words, the region was broadly self-sufficient. Europe's net imports of pulpwood in 1964, however, amounted to as much as 4.4 million cubic metres, which is equivalent to rather more than one million tons of paper and paperboard--approximately 3.4 per cent of Europe's total consumption in that year. On this analysis, there-fore, Europe joins Latin America, Africa, Asia, and the Pacific Area as a deficit region, leaving only two regions--North America and the U.S.S.R.--to meet the growing imbalance in the rest of the world.

In broad outline, the over-all regional deficits and surpluses in paper and paperboard, woodpulp, and pulpwood which existed in 1964, expressed in terms of woodpulp equivalent, were as follows:

Deficit Regions (million tons)		Surplus Regions (million tons)	
Europe	1.1	U.S.S.R.	1.2
Latin America	1.5	North America	5.1
Africa	0.4		
Asia	2.1		
Pacific Area	0.5		
	5.6		6.3

It will be noted that the sum of the surplus regions' net exports is greater than the deficit regions' total net imports--reflecting the fact that in any given year the leads and lags of international trade result in a higher level of recorded exports than imports. Regard-less of this statistical discrepancy, however, this analysis of the regional pattern of supply and demand is interesting in that it reveals the broad magnitude of regional surpluses and deficits, and, in addition, indicates the over-all significance of the imbalance. Thus in 1964, the aggregate regional imbalance of around 6 million tons of woodpulp equivalent represented something of the order of 5 per cent of the world's total consumption of woodpulp in the form of paper and paperboard, fibreboard and dissolving pulp.

CHAPTER **5** THE PROBABLE
LEVEL OF FUTURE
REQUIREMENTS

This chapter attempts to determine the probable future volume
of woodpulp requirements, both globally and regionally.   The data
it presents are based on the FAO estimates outlined earlier in this
study of the levels of consumption of paper and paperboard, dissolving pulp, and fibreboard likely to be attained by 1975.

For the principal end product, paper and paperboard, it will
be recalled that the FAO envisages a sharp increase in world
consumption from around 101. 5 million tons in 1964 to 178. 6 million
tons in 1975.   Even if it is assumed that the average input of woodpulp to produce 1 ton of paper remains entirely unchanged at
around 1. 07 tons over this period, however, it does not necessarily
follow that there will be a comparable expansion--of about 76 per
cent--in the demand for papermaking grades of woodpulp.   There
are, of course, two other important categories of raw materials
used in the production of paper and paperboard, and over a period
of time it is possible for the relative importance of each to change
significantly.

In 1964, about 77 per cent of the fibrous raw materials used in
the production of paper and paperboard consisted of woodpulp; a
further 18 per cent was made up of recovered waste paper; while
the remaining 5 per cent consisted of a variety of non-wood fibres,
such as bagasse, bamboo, esparto grass, reeds, straw,and sisal.

The use of waste paper is particularly significant in Europe and
North America, although there are signs, however, of some levelling
off in the relative importance of this raw material.   This is primarily
due to increasing costs of recovery and processing, but it also
reflects the growing incidence of non-recoverable and non-pulpable
paper--following the rapid expansion in usage of household and
toilet tissues, and the increasing presence of pernicious contraries
with the development of a wide range of plastic-laminated grades of
paper, paperboard, and converted products.   The rate of recovery
in North America and Europe is nevertheless expected to be broadly
maintained in the period up to 1975, and estimates recently prepared

by the FAO suggest that waste paper recovery rates throughout the
remaining regions of the world will improve along the lines set out
in Table 30.   The improvement will, in turn, result largely from
rising consumption and also from some slight movement towards
a decentralisation of the world's paper industry.

TABLE 30

Estimated Waste Paper Recovery Rates
(per cent of paper consumption)

	1955	1965	1975
Western Europe	25	25	25
Eastern Europe	22	23	24
U.S.S.R.	14	16	18
North America	26	26	26
Latin America	20	21	23
Africa	9	10	12
Near and Middle East	8	9	10
Far East (excluding Japan and Mainland China)	17	18	18
Japan	25	28	29
Mainland China	12	14	16
Oceania	12	12	12

In view of the fact that the recovery rate in the two major
consuming regions of North America and Europe is expected to be
maintained, while an improvement is anticipated in most of the
remaining geographical regions, waste paper will tend to account
for a growing proportion of the total volume of fibrous raw materials
used by the world's paper industry in the period up to 1975.

Relating the projected recovery rates set out in Table 30 to
the estimated paper and paperboard consumption in each geographical
region in 1975 suggests that the total volume of waste paper recovered for further use will be of the order of 42.6 million tons. On
the basis of an average yield of 85 per cent, this represents the
equivalent of 36.2 million tons of new paper and paperboard.   In
terms of a projected world consumption of 178.6 million tons of
paper and paperboard in 1975, waste paper would therefore account
for about 20 per cent of total fibrous raw material requirements--
compared with around 18 per cent in 1964.

As noted above, non-wood pulp represented some 5 per cent of the paper industry's aggregate requirements of fibrous raw materials in 1964.   Since a significant part of the world's expansion in paper consumption is expected to take place in regions which are deficient of adequate supplies of papermaking species of timber, the importance of non-wood fibrous materials will probably tend to grow slightly in coming years.   In general, however, they are perhaps unlikely to account for more than, say, 6 per cent of total fibrous raw material requirements for papermaking by 1975, as a very large proportion of total pulp output will continue to be produced by regions enjoying a plentiful supply of timber.   This would leave a balance of around 74 per cent of total supplies of papermaking fibres to be met by woodpulp, and hence it is assumed that the supply pattern is likely to be along the following lines in 1975.

TABLE 31

Projected Input of Fibrous Papermaking Material
in 1975 (end-product equivalent)

	Million Tons	Percentage Share
Woodpulp	131. 7	74
Waste paper	36. 2	20
Non-wood fibres	10. 7	6
Projected level of paper and paper-board production	178. 6	100

On the assumption that the average input of woodpulp per ton of paper averages 1. 07 tons in 1975, then woodpulp requirements for papermaking in that year are expected to be of the order of 141 million tons.   On top of this, the FAO anticipates that production of dissolving pulp will have reached 6. 4 million tons in 1975, and that consumption of fibreboard will be around 12. 2 million tons-- equivalent to about 7. 6 million tons of mechanical woodpulp on the basis of a conversion factor of 0. 62 tons of woodpulp to one ton of fibreboard.

TABLE 32

Estimated Global Demand for Woodpulp in 1975 (million tons)

	1964	1975
Papermaking grades)	83. 4	140. 9
Dissolving pulp)		6. 4
Fibreboard	4. 0	7. 6
	87. 4	154. 9

Thus, on the basis of the foregoing assumptions, global demand
for all grades of woodpulp in its three applications is expected to
reach some 155 million tons in 1975.   Paper and paperboard should
account for about 91 per cent of aggregate demand and dissolving
pulp for around 4 per cent, with the remaining 5 per cent being used
in the production of fibreboard.   This volume of aggregate demand
is equivalent to an increase of over 77 per cent when compared with
consumption in 1964.   Although this represents a slightly slower
rate of growth--one of just under 5.5 per cent per annum--than was
recorded in the previous decade, the increased demands placed upon
the world's forest resources in absolute terms are of course considerably greater.   The growth in woodpulp requirements between
1954 and 1964 was rather less than 39 million tons, but an expansion
in demand of almost exactly twice this magnitude is anticipated during
the period from 1964 to 1975.

Within the total projected output of around 141 million tons of
woodpulp for papermaking in 1975, there is likely to be a continuation
of the trend, evident over the past decade or more, for production
of chemical woodpulp to advance considerably faster than output of
mechanical grades.   Much of the absolute increase in the quantities
of paper and paperboard consumed in the years up to 1975 will be
accounted for by the developed countries, and a large and growing
proportion of this is likely to consist of industrial papers and paperboards.   Global usage of these grades in volume terms is therefore
expected to expand considerably more than consumption of printing
and writing papers and newsprint.   Since the main application of
mechanical pulp is in the latter category, while chemical pulp's
principal outlet is in the industrial paper and paperboard sector, the
share of the mechanical grades in total woodpulp output will fall
further in coming years.   The decline is likely to proceed, however,
more slowly than in the period from 1954 to 1964--during which time
mechanical pulp's share fell from 34.1 to 27.7 per cent.   By 1975
mechanical pulp is expected to account for no more than 25 per cent
of total woodpulp output.   The volume of output of mechanical grades
of papermaking woodpulp at that time might therefore be around 35
million tons (plus a further 7.6 million tons used in the manufacture
of fibreboard), with production of chemical woodpulp, including the
dissolving grades, being in the region of 112 million tons.

Turning now to an analysis of the FAO forecasts of the regional
pattern of paper and paperboard consumption in 1975, one of the most
important questions to examine is this: are the deficit regions
likely to attain greater self-sufficiency, or will they tend to become
even more dependent on those regions which produce a net exportable

TABLE 33

Projected Levels of Paper and Paperboard Consumption and the Industry's Fibrous Raw Material Requirements in 1975 (million tons)

	Consumption of Paper and Paperboard	Waste Paper Recovery Rate (per cent)	Waste Paper Supplies	Waste Paper Consumption (Paper Equivalent)*	Balance of Requirements of Fibrous Materials (Paper Equivalent)
Europe	55.8	25	13.8	11.8	44.0
U.S.S.R.	16.5	18	3.0	2.6	13.9
North America	62.2	26	16.2	13.8	48.4
Latin America	7.6	23	1.7	1.4	6.2
Africa	2.8	12	0.3	0.25	2.55
Asia	31.3	23	7.2	6.1	25.2
Pacific Area	2.4	12	0.3	0.25	2.15
World Total	178.6	24	42.6	36.2	142.4

* Based on a waste paper yield of 85 per cent.

surplus of woodpulp. The FAO forecast envisages world consumption of paper and paperboard reaching a level of 178.6 million tons in 1975, and the regional pattern of consumption inherent in this projection is shown in Table 33, together with the expected waste paper recovery rates likely to be attained and the balance of virgin fibrous raw material requirements for this sector.

The figures shown in the last column of Table 33 represent the balance of paper and paperboard consumption which will be based on either woodpulp or non-wood fibres, since the contribution of waste paper to new paper supply has already been taken into account.   It is difficult to assess the probable future pattern of regional usage of non-wood fibrous material, which in any case forms a relatively small proportion of total papermaking requirements.   Earlier in this chapter it was suggested that the contribution of non-wood fibres to total papermaking materials, which amounted to some 5 per cent in 1964, might be expected to grow slightly, achieving a share of around 6 per cent by 1975.   For the purposes of the present analysis it might not be reasonable to assume that the expansion in the volume of usage of non-wood fibres between 1964 and 1975 is comparable in each of the producing regions, so that the regional pattern of non-wood consumption is broadly the same in each year.   Once these relatively small volumes have been excluded, it is possible to gauge the outstanding balance of regional requirements of woodpulp inherent in the FAO projections of paper and paperboard consumption in 1975, on the basis of 1.07 tons of woodpulp being needed to produce one ton of paper or paperboard.

TABLE 34

Estimated Requirements of Woodpulp to Sustain the Levels
of Consumption of Paper and Paperboard, Dissolving
Pulp, and Fibreboard Forecast for 1975 (million tons)

	Production of Woodpulp in 1964*	Requirements of Woodpulp in 1975*	Increase 1964-75	
			Volume	Per-centage
Europe	25.1 (21.9)	49.3 (44.2)	24.2	90
U.S.S.R.	4.9 (4.2)	17.2 (14.8)	12.3	250
North America	47.7 (44.3)	53.9 (50.4)	6.2	13
Latin America	1.3 (1.15)	6.0 (5.6)	4.7	360
Africa	0.5 (0.25)	2.8 (2.5)	2.3	460
Asia	6.9 (6.1)	23.1 (21.1)	16.2	235
Pacific Area	1.0 (0.85)	2.6 (2.3)	1.6	160
World Total	87.4(78.75)	154.9 (140.9)	67.5	77

* Figures in parantheses represent papermaking pulp.

These figures are set out in Table 34, together with details of
aggregate production in 1964, and requirements in 1975, of papermaking and dissolving grades of woodpulp, and woodpulp used in the
manufacture of fibreboard.

It should be emphasised that the figures set out in the above
table in respect of aggregate regional requirements of papermaking
grades of woodpulp, dissolving pulp, and mechanical pulp used in the
manufacture of fibreboard in 1975 are not intended to represent a
forecast of the probable pattern of regional production of woodpulp
at that time.   They merely reveal the level of output which would be
necessary in order for each region to satisfy its own aggregate
derived demand for woodpulp.   They are based on the FAO projections of the regional pattern of consumption of paper and paperboard (with an allowance having been made for the probable contribution of waste paper and non-wood fibres to total requirements
of fibrous papermaking materials), dissolving pulp, and fibreboard
in 1975.

The table is nevertheless an extremely interesting one.   First,
it indicates the extent to which woodpulp production needs to be
raised in order for any particular region to achieve self-sufficiency
in 1975.   Secondly, it shows up the implications for the future
development of inter-regional trade in woodpulp or paper if it is
judged that the requirements of certain regions are clearly beyond
their capacity.   They might be so, for example, due to the lack of
adequate long-fibre raw materials or a shortage of capital to finance
industrial development of this nature.

Looking first at those regions which have in the past enjoyed
a considerable surplus of papermaking materials, one of the most
striking facts to emerge from Table 34 is that North America needs
to increase its output of woodpulp by only 13 per cent between 1964
and 1975 in order to be able to satisfy its domestic requirements
fully.   This region is clearly capable of achieving an expansion in
output several times greater than this modest increase, and will
therefore undoubtedly remain a major net exporter of woodpulp and
pulp-based products.   The U. S. S. R. , on the other hand, needs to
increase production of woodpulp by as much as 250 per cent between
1964 and 1975 in order to remain self-sufficient.   Yet there is
little doubt that this region will continue to be a significant source
of net exports in 1975, where necessary at the expense of an arti-
fically restrained level of domestic demand.   Russia possesses
immense untapped forest resources, and is directing all its energy
towards their rapid exploitation with the declared aim of overtaking

the Canadian level of chemical woodpulp output in the early 1970's.

European output of woodpulp needs to be raised by about 90 per cent in the period up to 1975 in order to meet the region's requirements.   At first sight, this appears to be a much more manageable rate of expansion than the 250 per cent increase which is required of the Russian woodpulp industry.   In volume terms, however, the increase called for in European output per year amounts to one of over 24 million tons--very nearly double the theoretical expansion involved in the U. S. S. R. which is at a very considerable advantage in having enormous reserves of timber.   An analysis of the likely future pattern of regional supplies of woodpulp is carried out in the following chapter, and hence at this point it will be sufficient to note that Europe is unlikely to be able to raise its woodpulp output by anything like this amount.   It is therefore expected that the region will move increasingly into deficit during the course of the next decade.

Considerably higher rates of growth in woodpulp output will be required in the remaining four geographical regions if the fairly substantial dependence on imported supplies of woodpulp and paper and paperboard which existed in 1964 is to be reduced, let alone eliminated, by 1975.   To achieve self-sufficiency in Africa, for example, production of woodpulp would need to be raised from about 0. 5 million tons in 1964 to around 2. 8 million tons in 1975--an increase of 460 per cent.   In Latin America an expansion in annual output of 4. 7 million tons, or 360 per cent, is involved, while in the Pacific Area production of woodpulp would need to be raised by 1. 4 million tons.   Finally, a rather more than twofold increase is called for in Asia, which is approximately the same order of magnitude as the expansion necessary in the U. S. S. R.   In volume terms, however, the margin between Asian woodpulp output in 1964 and requirements in 1975--at 16. 2 million tons--is significantly greater than in the U. S. S. R. which is also much more happily endowed with suitable papermaking species of timber.

CHAPTER **6** THE PROSPECTS
FOR SUPPLY

The previous chapter carried out a broad assessment, first, of
the probable volume of woodpulp requirements needed to attain the
levels of consumption of paper and paperboard, dissolving pulp, and
fibreboard projected for 1975, and secondly, of the extent to which
woodpulp production in each of the geographical regions under consideration must be raised in order to achieve a state of self-sufficiency.
The object of this chapter is to examine in general terms such
questions as the nature of regional forest resources, the development
of productive facilities, and the competing claims of other wood-
using sectors. From such a review it is possible to draw certain
inferences concerning, on the one hand, the extent to which the
principal deficit regions are likely either to reduce or to increase
their dependence on extra-regional supplies and, on the other hand,
the likelihood of the present surplus regions playing a growing or a
declining role in net trade in woodpulp.

As a first step, it may be interesting to consider briefly the
regional distribution of the world's forest resources. Table 35
sets out details of the total forest area in each of the main geographical
regions, the proportion of the land area covered by forests, and a
comparison of the regional distribution of both the world forest area
and the world population.

From this table it can be seen that the world's forests in total
cover something like 10.4 million acres, which represents little
short of one third of the world's total land area. The regional
forest data shown in this table reveal as one of the main facts that
only in Asia and Europe is there a sharp adverse disparity between
a region's share of the world's forest area and its share of the
world's population. In each of the remaining five principal geographical regions, on the other hand, there is a positive relationship between these two aggregates. Thus, the U.S.S.R. for
example, which accounted for 7.0 per cent of the world's population
in 1964, contains 21.5 per cent of the global forest area, while an
almost equally advantageous relationship is enjoyed by the North
America region.

TABLE 35

Selected Features of the World's Forest Resources

	Total Forest Area (million acres)	Forests as a Proportion of Total Land Area (%)	Forest Composition			Proportion of World Forest Area (%)	World Population 1964 (%)
			Coniferous (%)	Broad-leaved (%)	Mixed (%)		
Europe	417	30.4	53	37	10	4.0	13.4
U.S.S.R.	2,246	40.6	76	24	–	21.5	7.0
North America	1,854	38.8	55	32	13	17.7	6.4
Latin America	2,152	42.6	1	94	5	20.6	7.1
Africa	1,885	25.4	1	98	1	18.0	9.3
Asia	1,355	37.9	*	*	*	13.0	56.3
Near East	22	1.6	10	86	4	0.2	2.3
Far East	1,095	44.7	7	72	21	10.5	32.0
Mainland China	238	9.8	*	*	*	2.3	22.0
Pacific Area	539	27.2	36	14	50	5.2	0.5
World Total	10,448	32.2	35	60	5	100.0	100.0

* Not available.

Note: The data in this table, which relate to the position in the early 1960's, are not fully comparable due to variations in coverage and definitions.

68

The needs of the industries producing pulp-based products do
not, of course, represent the sole demand placed upon the world's
forest resources, nor even the most important element of aggregate
demand for timber. The following table gives an indication of the
relative importance of the main applications and the trend in each
sector between 1951 and 1963.

TABLE 36

Principal Applications of Global Roundwood
Production (million cubic metres)

	1951	1963	Percentage Share 1951	1963	Percentage Change 1951-63
Sawlogs, veneer logs, and logs for sleepers	493.4	656.7	29.5	34.2	+33
Pulpwood, pit-props, and roundwood used in the manufacture of particle board and fibreboard	185.6	257.1	11.1	13.4	+39
Other industrial wood	129.2	118.2	7.7	6.2	- 9
Fuelwood	865.6	886.5	51.7	46.2	+ 2
	1,673.8	1,918.5	100.0	100.0	+15

In 1963, recorded world production of roundwood amounted to
rather more than 1.9 billion cubic metres. Of this total, the category from which woodpulp is derived (which also, however, includes
pitprops and wood used in the manufacture of particle board, which
serves to inflate the total somewhat) accounted for more than 13.4
per cent. The main element of demand for the world's output of
timber is in fact provided by fuelwood requirements. These accounted for little short of half of global supplies of roundwood in 1963,
and probably account for a similar proportion now. The principal
demand for industrial wood stems from the sawmilling sector. In
1963 sawlogs, veneer logs and logs for sleepers absorbed rather
more than one third of total roundwood production in that year, with
the remaining 6.2 per cent of output being used in other industrial
applications.

During the years from 1951 to 1963, however, there have been several interesting developments within the main wood-using sectors. Total roundwood supplies in that period rose by about 15 per cent-- equivalent to a rate of growth of rather less than 1 per cent a year. Within this slowly expanding aggregate supply situation, however, a much greater increase in demand emerged for industrial wood than for fuelwood. Requirements for fuelwood rose, in fact, by only 2 per cent between 1951 and 1963, and although this outlet still accounts for the bulk of roundwood usage, its share has nevertheless fallen from 51.7 per cent to 46.2 per cent. On the other hand, the demand for industrial wood of all types rose between 1951 and 1963 from 808 to 1,032 million cubic metres, or by nearly 28 per cent. The sharpest rate of expansion within this over-all category took place in the pulpwood sector, where consumption rose by some 39 per cent. The sawlog sector achieved a slightly less rapid rate of growth amounting to about one third, but, on the other hand, the group of industries this sector embraces is a very much larger outlet for wood than the pulpwood sector, using about two and a half times as much in 1963. Again, the relative positions of the sectors reviewed are unlikely to have changed substantially between 1963 and the present time.

Although aggregate world consumption of roundwood is divided almost equally between industrial requirements and fuelwood demand, there are very marked variations in the pattern of usage among the different regions. These are illustrated in Table 37, which sets out details of the regional breakdown of global usage of roundwood and the share of regional consumption accounted for by fuelwood and industrial wood.

TABLE 37

Estimated Regional Wood Usage in 1960-62

	Percentage Share of Global Wood Consumption	Percentage Share Industrial Wood	Fuelwood
Europe	16.6	70	30
U.S.S.R.	16.5	71	29
North America	16.7	87	13
Latin America	10.8	17	83
Africa	9.7	11	89
Asia) Pacific Area)	29.7	28	72

There are a number of interesting points revealed by this table.
On the one hand, it shows that the individual shares of aggregate
world consumption of roundwood accounted for by Europe, the
U.S.S.R., and North America were virtually identical in 1960-62.
On the other hand, the table highlights the very much larger share
of global wood usage held by Asia and the Pacific Area, which, at
nearly 30 per cent, was not far short of double the level of consumption in the three main pulp-producing regions.   This is perhaps
surprising if one bears in mind the very much smaller level of pulp
production in Asia and the Pacific Area, although this could of course
be offset to some extent by a relatively higher volume of output in
the other wood-using industries.   The explanation is to be seen,
however, in the last two columns of Table 37.   These show that
between 70 and 87 per cent of total demand for roundwood is derived
from the industrial sector in Europe, the U.S.S.R., and North
America.   In Asia and the Pacific Area, however, the emphasis
is almost exactly reversed, with only 28 per cent of the total con-
sisting of industrial wood and as much as 72 per cent of wood being
used in its raw form as fuelwood.   In the remaining two regions--
Latin America and Africa-- the relative importance of fuelwood is
even greater.   Only 17 per cent and 11 per cent of total demand
respectively, stems from the industrial wood-using sector.

On the basis of the assumptions concerning income growth outlined in Chapter 1, the FAO has recently estimated that between
1963 and 1975 world requirements of wood are likely to rise by little
short of one quarter to a level approaching 2.5 billion cubic metres.
Within this aggregate expansion, however, there is expected to be a
continuing steady growth in the use of wood as an industrial raw
material rather than as a fuel or for use in its raw state.   Thus,
although a large proportion of total consumption will continue to be
accounted for by fuelwood and constructional requirements, most of
the expansion in usage will come from its growing industrial application.   This is doubtless a step in the right direction and one that
might be expected to be taken by a world progressing towards greater
industrialisation and rising living standards.

An indication of the relative trends anticipated in the main uses
is given in the following table.   Total roundwood requirements
during the 1963-75 period are expected to increase at a rate some
65 per cent faster than the expansion recorded over the previous
twelve years.   Within this total two opposite trends are likely to
occur.   There should be a below-average growth in the demand for
fuelwood leading to a slight decline in the share of roundwood used
in this application, and a corresponding increase in the proportion

TABLE 38

Estimated Developments in Global Consumption
of Roundwood

	Percentage Change	
	1951-63	1963-1975
Sawlogs, veneer logs, and logs for sleepers	+33	+ 28
Pulpwood, pitprops, and round-wood used in the manufacture of particle board and fibre-board	+39	+117
Other industrial wood	- 9	- 6
Fuelwood	+ 2	+ 10
	+15	+ 25

of total output used for industrial purposes --from less than 54 per cent in 1963 to more than 55 per cent in 1975. In the industrial wood sector, however, little more than an average increase in demand is expected for sawlogs, together with a fall in absolute terms. in the use of other industrial wood. This means that far and away the largest expansion, both in absolute and proportionate terms, is looked for in the pulpwood sector. Here, it is envisaged that demand will more than double, raising this sector's share of total roundwood usage from around 13.4 per cent in 1963 to about 18.3 per cent in 1975, and its share of industrial wood requirements from approximately one quarter to one third over the same period.

It may be interesting to note that such a development in the pattern of demand has important implications for the wood-producing sector. Pulpwood is usually obtained from the smaller or poorer qualities of roundwood and also from wood residues. Hence there will need to be an appropriate over-all shift in emphasis towards the supply of adequate quantities, in place of the greater attention which has previously been paid to quality, form, and size, in view of the relative importance of the sawnwood sector hitherto.

Returning now to a consideration of the statistics of forest resources set out earlier in this chapter, it is clear that while they are of value in providing a broad perspective of the distribution of the world's forest reserves, these bald figures take no account of such factors as regional variations in growing stock, yields, access-ibility and, of particular importance, differences in the composition of the forest area by the main species. Due to a combination of technical and locational factors, the traditional species of timber

used in the manufacture of woodpulp have largely consisted of coniferous varieties. Hence, Northern Europe, the U.S.S.R., and
North America are particularly well endowed with resources to
produce woodpulp on a large scale. A wide belt of heavily conifer-
ous-forested land which is readily accessible runs across the north
of each of these regions. In the U.S.S.R., coniferous forests
account for rather more thanthree quarters of the total forest area,
while in North America and Europe a somewhat lower, but nevertheless sizable, share of the total forest area is made up of
coniferous species. At the other extreme, a mere 1 per cent of the
forest area of both the Latin American and the African region con-
sists of coniferous timber, although the former has a further 5 per
cent in the form of mixed coniferous and broadleaved timber.

One of the most significant trends which has taken place in the
pulp and paper industry in recent years, however, and one which
has far-reaching implications for the regional pattern of woodpulp
production in the future, is the growing usage of broadleaved species
of timber. The commercial exploitation of these species for pulping follow the development of improved pulping processes and the
introduction of new pulping techniques. The pulp and paper industry
has traditionally been dependent on coniferous species. Because
of their long fibres they impart strength to the paper, and they are
easily pulped with the traditional technology. As a result, pulp
mills have sprung up mainly in areas that have access to supplies
of coniferous timber. The advent of new sulphate and semi-chemical
pulping processes, however, has enabled raw material usage to
be extended to include a number of broadleaved species.

TABLE 39

World Supply Pattern of Fibrous Raw Materials for Papermaking and Dissolving Grades of Pulp in 1961 (per cent)

	Coniferous Woodpulp	Broadleaved Woodpulp	Non-Wood Pulp
Europe	83	10	7
U.S.S.R.	99	1	-
North America	83	16	1
Latin America	53	14	33
Africa	17	63	20
Asia	41	30	29
Pacific Area	43	57	-
World Total	78	16	6

Clearly, the incentive to maximise the use of broadleaved species in pulping is greatest in those areas which have a significant proportion of their timber resources in the form of non-coniferous species. Thus, as can be seen from Table 39, the contribution to total pulp production made by broadleaved species in the U.S.S.R., Europe,and North America ranged from 1 per cent up to 16 per cent in 1961. On the other hand, in Asia, Africa,and the Pacific Area broadleaved species accounted for between around one third and two

TABLE 40

Actual and Projected Usage of Broadleaved Species in the
Production of Papermaking and Dissolving Grades
of Woodpulp (million cubic metres)

| | Pulpwood Production | | Broadleaved Pulpwood |
	Total	Broadleaved	as a % of the Total
U.S.A.			
1950	45.5	6.4	14
1962	94.2	19.6	21
1970	124.3	29.7	24
1980	169.4	46.2	27
Japan			
1956	8.6	1.3	15
1961	14.2	4.6	32
U.S.S.R.			
1963	16.5	0.3	2
1965	20.7	1.0	5
1975	56.3	8.6	15
Western Europe			
1950	27.5	1.2	4
1960	52.3	5.3	10
1975	90.0	20.6	23
Scandinavian Countries			
1950	22.7	0.6	3
1960	40.1	2.0	5
1975	57.6	8.6	15
Other Western European Countries			
1950	4.8	0.6	13
1960	12.2	3.3	27
1975	32.4	12.0	37

thirds of total virgin fibrous raw materials and an even larger proportion of timber used for pulping in the first two regions.

A very considerable extension in the use of broadleaved species
is anticipated in a number of the major pulp-producing areas over
the next decade or so.   Thus, the proportion of broadleaved timber
is expected to rise to over one quarter of total pulpwood output in
the United States by 1980, while in both the U.S.S.R. and the Scandinavian countries it is envisaged that broadleaved pulpwood's contribution to aggregate proportion will expand to around 15 per cent
by 1975.

Among the main problems arising from the need to increase
usage of short-fibred broadleaved pulps is the question of their
adaptability to high-speed machines, and also their suitability for
the production of a number of grades of paper and paperboard.
Happily these problems are being overcome.   In certain cases,
broadleaved pulps from a number of species have been found to
produce a better brightness and opacity than corresponding coniferous
pulps--characteristics of particular advantage for cultural papers.
Similarly, broadleaved pulps have been found to yield a more uniform texture and better surface for printing papers than long-fibred
pulps.   Thus, with modern high-speed machinery it is now possible
to make printing papers from a 100 per cent broadleaved pulp fur-
nish.   As far as packaging grades of paper and paperboard are concerned, the bulk of high-strength wrapping continues to be made
from unbleached coniferous sulphate pulp.   Nevertheless, broadleaved pulps are particularly suitable for making high-yield pulps
for glassine and greaseproof paper and are superior to coniferous
pulps in the production of corrugating medium.

From the technical point of view, therefore, broadleaved pulp
is capable of making a growing contribution to total woodpulp requirements in the major producing areas.   The principal contributing
factors conducive to the use of more broadleaved timber include
some pressure on supplies of coniferous pulpwood and, consequently,
its rising cost.   Although logging and handling costs tend to be
higher per unit of raw material for broadleaved species than for
coniferous species at the present time, delivered costs for hardwood pulpwood still tend to be lower owing to lower prices of the
standing timber. It may be anticipated, however, that as the demand
for hardwood gathers momentum in coming years this price differential will tend to narrow.

At the present time the hardwoods from the enormous areas of

tropical rain forest have hardly been used for pulping. With the
development of new pulping techniques the obstacles here are less
of a technological nature, since many species have been successfully pulped under laboratory conditions, than of an economic nature.
The necessary process of presorting a crop as heterogeneous in its
properties as the tropical rain forest tends to be costly. There
are, however, a few examples of successful commercial operations
utilising tropical species. Thus, there are now mills in Colombia
and Brazil pulping mixed tropical hardwood, and a number of mills--
in Pakistan and India, for example--utilising single species.

Another significant factor in appraising the potential pattern of
regional supplies of woodpulp is the establishment of plantation-
grown pulpwood. The planting of forest trees is, of course, by no
means a new phenomenon. It has long been used to supplement
natural resources, for example, and to extend or create forests for
productive or protective purposes. Planting has also been undertaken in order to replace with different species forest resources
which were generally inadequate from a qualitative point of view.

In recent years, however, greater emphasis has come to be
placed on more intensive afforestation. Various measures of soil
working, fertiliser application, and irrigation are being adopted to
make the environment more suitable for high-yielding species.
These measures, together with the application of policies of accelera-
ted cultivation, have been successful in raising yields very considerably in certain instances. Thus from man-made pine forests it has
become possible to produce pulpwood within a period of around ten
years.

Man-made forests, which provide homogeneous raw materials,
with short rotations and high unit yields, have been extended greatly
in recent years in a large number of countries throughout the world.
Among them are Chile, Brazil, New Zealand, Australia, West
Germany, the U.K., and South Africa. As a result, man-made
forests now represent an important part of the world's productive
forest resources, and make a contribution to wood requirements
very much in excess of their share of the global forest area. There
are nevertheless a number of factors which will tend to limit the
extent to which man-made forests can continue to increase this contribution. For example, the susceptibility of large areas of a
single species of timber to epidemic attacks from insects and
diseases increases with the departure from natural growing conditions and environmental factors. In addition, there has so far been
little success in finding suitable species for certain areas where the

need for supplementary supplies of timber is particularly great--
in the dry savanna areas, for example.

Notwithstanding these limitations, the growing development of
plantation wood for pulping purposes, together with the application
of satisfactory techniques for pulping broadleaved species of timber,
have been instrumental in providing some means of redressing the
sharp regional imbalance in the more traditional pulping species.
Yet there are two important points that need to be considered.
First, an over-all assessment of the world's forest resources con-
ceals the fact that much of the forest area in certain regions--in
Western Africa, for example-- is of a low-yielding type. Secondly,
and in addition, a severe inadequacy in the natural forest resources
afflicts the more heavily populated areas of the world. This is
particularly true of such areas as Northern Africa and the Near
East, large parts of Southern Asia and mainland China. Since these
areas account for around one third of the world's population, consumption of wood is accordingly restricted.

As far as mainland China is concerned, however, a vast planting effort has been taking place during the past decade. Plans for
250 million acres to be planted between 1956 and 1967 were origin-
ally laid down, and it is possible that something between one third
and two thirds of this undertaking was achieved by the end of the
1950's. Survival rates may have been less than satisfactory, but
if this effort is sustained the results will subsequently transform
the wood supply situation in mainland China.

In Japan, the sharp increase in woodpulp requirements which
has followed the spectacular leap ahead of the economy during the
past decade or so has led to a growing dependence on imported
supplies of raw materials. Efforts are accordingly being made to
develop the country's indigenous timber resources. A considerable
volume of planting has been undertaken, taking the form in the main
of replacing overmature stands and small areas of forest unsuitable
for commercial exploitation with high-yielding species. Man-made
forests already account for much of Japan's forests. There are
plans to extend plantations in the period up to 1975 to the point where
they represent around 40 per cent of the total forest area.

Signs of a continuing imbalance between the country's demand
for woodpulp and the domestic raw material supply, however, are
unmistakable. Japanese pulp and paper interests are, therefore,
making sizable investments in the North American forestry sector.
A rising volume of trade between Japan and North America can

accordingly be anticipated in coming years.   On the basis of the
FAO's most recent projections, Japan's pulpwood needs in 1975
will be of the order of 42.5 million cubic metres of roundwood
equivalent, of which little more than three quarters will be met by
domestic supplies of roundwood and wood residues.   Net imports
of pulpwood, woodpulp, or paper and paperboard are therefore
expected to expand dramatically to around 10 million cubic metres
of roundwood equivalent by 1975.

In Africa, a considerable increase in the production of woodpulp
has in fact been achieved in recent years in Northern and Southern
Africa, the two sub-regions which account for the bulk of output.
Furthermore, a significant part of the region's expansion in woodpulp production over the past decade or so has been based on the
successful development of fast-growing pine plantations, and plans
for establishing further productive capacity based on plantation-
grown pulpwood are being actively explored in various parts of the
continent.

For Africa as a whole, the FAO estimates suggest that production of pulp of all types is likely to reach around 2 million tons by
1975, with nearly half being contributed by the southern sub-region.
This compares with a regional output of rather less than half a
million tons in 1964, of which nearly 20 per cent consisted of pulp
produced from non-wood fibres.   If it is assumed that a similar
ratio between woodpulp and non-wood fibre pulp exists in 1975, output of the former would amount to about 1.6 million tons.   This
falls some way short, however, of the estimated level of Africa's
internal woodpulp requirements, which were calculated earlier in
this study as amounting to around 2.8 million tons.   Thus, in spite
of the very rapid development of productive capacity anticipated in
this region over the next few years, Africa's dependence on outside
supplies of woodpulp equivalent in net terms is expected to rise from
about 0.4 million tons in 1964 to probably well over 1 million tons in
1975.

The future supply potential in Latin America varies considerably
between different parts of the continent.   On the one hand, the
Caribbean islands have very limited forest resources, while countries such as Argentina and Paraguay have large forests but very
little coniferous timber.   On the other hand, Brazil has vast forest
reserves and hence the potential to remain a significant exporter of
wood products, while the extensive area of natural and planted
coniferous timber in Chile is likely to be reflected in a growing
volume of exports in coming years.

In general, Latin America has the raw material resources to enable it to supply all of its domestic requirements of pulp products for as far ahead as one cares to look. Yet at the present time it is dependent on net imports because it lacks adequate manufacturing facilities, and is handicapped by the inaccessibility of much of the forest area. Apart from lacking technical skills, the Latin American pulp and paper industry is also short of capital. The industry is, of course, particularly capital-intensive, and an enormous volume of investment will be necessary if the potential which Latin America has in its forests is to be adequately harnessed to supply domestic requirements, let alone the export demand which it is physically capable of meeting from the available raw material stock. Since Latin America is at an early stage of economic and industrial development, it is inevitably subject to many competing demands on the limited capital available. It is therefore considered unlikely that enough mills will be installed in the years up to 1975 to enable anything like self-sufficiency in woodpulp to be achieved. Thus, although certain Latin American countries, such as Chile, will probably develop a growing export trade over this period, the region as a whole is expected to remain fairly heavily dependent on imports from other parts of the world during the foreseeable future.

The transition in Europe from being a net exporter to becoming a net importer during the past decade was pointed out earlier in this study. Growing raw material limitations are evident in the principal pulp and paper supplying countries of Northern Europe. The exportable surplus of some of the smaller European suppliers, moreover, may well disappear in the face of sharply rising indigenous requirements. Hence a rapid expansion in Europe's net imports of timber from other parts of the world is envisaged in the years up to 1975. By the end of this period, it has been estimated that Europe's net imports of pulpwood, woodpulp, or paper and paperboard will have risen to somewhere between 20 and 30 million cubic metres of roundwood equivalent, mainly accounted for by growing deficiencies in the U.K. and the EEC countries. On the basis of an assumed average of 4 cubic metres of roundwood to 1 ton of woodpulp, this volume of net imports may be taken to be equivalent to between 5 and 7.5 million tons of pulp. In broad terms this represents around 10-15 per cent of Europe's estimated total woodpulp requirements in 1975. Hence, this region's net dependence on outside supplies will increase quite markedly. It has been calculated that, in 1964, taking into account the positive balance in Europe's regional trade in paper and paperboard, its net reliance on imports represented only some 3-4 per cent of aggregate consumption.

Nor is this trend towards a growing dependence on outside supplies likely to be reversed in the foreseeable future. A combination of forestry improvement policies, large-scale afforestation measures,and an increasing emphasis on quick-growing species can undoubtedly serve to raise Europe's output of timber substantially. But in the period up to 1975 and, in particular, beyond this date, it is unlikely that this expansion will be capable of accommodating more than a part of the continued advance in requirements. Furthermore, Europe may tend to find itself at an increasing disadvantage in terms of timber production costs with certain other parts of the world where there are resources yet to be brought into use, and where more favourable climatic and soil conditions are enjoyed.

In the Pacific Area, the past pattern of supply has taken the form of a growing volume of woodpulp exports from New Zealand to Australia which has, however, been inadequate to close the widening gap between domestic production and aggregate requirements in Australia. As a result, the Pacific Area as a whole had become a significant deficit region by 1964, particularly in long-fibred pulp. This situation is unlikely to be reversed in the years up to 1975. The reason is to be found in New Zealand's inability to continue to raise output from its existing coniferous resources and in Australia's dependence on imports of long-fibred pulp, for much of its output is of hardwood pulp, mainly eucalyptic.

Although it is difficult to be precise about the specific quantities likely to be involved, the general outlook for the period up to 1975 is for a continuing deficit in aggregate domestic requirements of papermaking and dissolving grades of woodpulp, and pulp used in the manufacture of fibreboard, in each of the five geographical regions-- Asia, Africa, Latin America, Europe,and the Pacific Area--which were dependent on net imported supplies in 1964. Europe, however, is likely to experience the largest widening in the imbalance between regional supply and demand, both in proportionate and in absolute terms.

As in the past, the avoidance of constraints in the natural growth in consumption of pulp-based products in the deficit regions will require an appropriate continuation and expansion in the net exporting capabilities of the two surplus regions of North America and the U.S.S.R. In general, it is envisaged that these two regions will have little difficulty in meeting the additional demands placed upon them in the period up to 1975, or in fact some way beyond this date. However, there is likely to be something of a shift in emphasis, with the U.S.S.R. gaining in relative importance as a net exporter,

despite the very sharp rise envisaged in its own internal woodpulp
requirements over the next decade.

Throughout much of the period under consideration, however,
Canada will continue to dominate the international scene, certainly
in inter-regional flows of woodpulp.   Such countries as Sweden,
Finland,and Norway will of course remain large exporters of woodpulp and paper. and paperboard.   Again, the main direction of their
trade flows will continue to be towards the major deficit areas within
their own region--the U.K. and the EEC countries.   Canada in any
case possesses a much greater proportionate and absolute scope for
expanding its output and it now caters less for the U.S. paper industry
than it did.   An examination of the past pattern of trade reveals that
a growing share of its rising volume of exports has been destined
for markets other than the United States.   Thus in extra-regional
terms, North America is expected to contribute a major proportion
of the growth in woodpulp trade which will take place in coming years.
In 1964 well over 25 per cent of Canada's woodpulp output of 13.7
million tons was being exported and North American net exports
amounted to around 2.2 million tons.   With output in Canada expected to very nearly double by 1975 it is clear that it will be capable
of accommodating substantial additional extra-regional demands.

By the early 1970's, however, the U.S.S.R. is likely to be making
a growing contribution to the alleviation of deficiencies in domestic
woodpulp supplies in other parts of the world.   Russia enjoys an
enormous potential in this respect.   Its forest area is well in excess
of that of Canada, the United States, and Northern Europe combined.
Its growing stock is nearly double that possessed by these three
regions together.   There is, however, a much smaller differential
between the total net annual growth in the U.S.S.R. and in North
America and the Nordic countries, due to the existence of large
areas of mature and over-mature timber in Russia.

In spite of this favourable relationship in potential raw material
supplies, Russia's total softwood removals in the early 1960's were
somewhat below those of North America, and only slightly higher
than European removals.   Furthermore, a much higher proportion
of the U.S.S.R.'s timber supplies is used for fuelwood than is the
case, for example, in North America--over 28 per cent during the
1960-62 period compared with less than 12 per cent in North
America.

At the Twenty-third Congress of the CPSU, which outlined the
five-year economic development plan for the 1966-70 period, pro-

vision was made for production of woodpulp to be raised from around
3.5 million tons in 1965 to between about 9 and 10 million tons in
1970.   Thereafter, the development of the Russian pulp industry is
much more conjectural.   It is known, however, that Russia's ultimate
aim is to rival Canada as a producer of chemical woodpulp during
the 1970's, and to become a major exporter of bleached sulphate
pulp.

Much of the expansion in forest industry capacity being carried
out or planned in the Soviet Union at the present time takes the form
of a number of vast, fully-integrated complexes.   Some of the big-
gest are designed to produce woodpulp in quantities of up to a million
tons a year, together with large quantities of sawnwood, particle
board, furniture, etc.   The much greater degree of integration
which is thereby becoming a feature of the Russian forest industry
is likely to be reflected in a change in the form in which exports are
made in coming years.   The sharp expansion in Russian exports of
pulpwood during the 1954-64 period was noted earlier in this study.
Over these years, in fact, the increase in Russian pulpwood exports
coincided with a marked decline in exports from other parts of the
world.   Pulpwood is clearly an expensive commodity to transport
over long distances, and with Russia rapidly expanding its pulping
capacity there is unlikely to be any significant or sustained increase
in world trade in pulpwood in future years.   A growing proportion
will accordingly be converted in the country of origin into woodpulp,
or paper and paperboard.

In the period up to 1975 there is judged to be considerable scope
for sharp increases in international and inter-regional trade in woodpulp and pulp-based products.   Growing deficiencies are most likely
to be experienced, not only in many individual important consuming
countries, but in five of the seven regions into which the world has
been divided for the purposes of this study.   It is difficult, however,
to gauge the extent to which this expansion in trade is likely to be
more marked for woodpulp or for paper and paperboard.   In general,
supplying countries clearly prefer to export a more highly processed
product, whereas importing countries, on the other hand, see their
interests as lying in the protection of their domestic paper and
paperboard industries by means of high tariffs on finished products
and, in many cases, the completely duty-free entry of papermaking
materials.

The probable outcome of these conflicting currents of national
interest in terms of the respective development of trade in woodpulp and paper and paperboard is hard to predict.   But a really

efficient international allocation and use of resources ought to transcend national considerations generally if not invariably. Thus, among the paper products, some of the mass-produced grades, such as newsprint and kraft liner, benefit very considerably from economies of large-scale production. In recent years there has been a tendency for their manufacture to become increasingly concentrated in large plants integrated with their woodpulp source, rather than being located near the final market. As a result, trade in such products may be expected to assume a growing importance in coming years, at the expense of the more specialised or less standardised grades of paper and paperboard. These grades are used in smaller quantities and the advantage enjoyed by the paper-maker's proximity to his market tends to offset or even outweigh his disadvantage of importing woodpulp and using it for a not fully-integrated operation.

The growth in international and inter-regional trade in wood-pulp, however, may nevertheless tend to outstrip the expansion which takes place in trade in paper and paperboard. It is feasible for regions and countries which are deficient in papermaking species of timber to develop their own non-integrated paper and paperboard industries. In addition, in spite of the clash of interests between would-be paper exporting countries and the deficit countries, the upper hand held by the importer should continue to be the determining factor. This is so because of the surplus in woodpulp which has existed in the world market during the past few years and which is likely to remain a feature of that market for perhaps the rest of this decade. Finally, the large volume of investment in production capacity made by Japanese and European interests in North America, and by North American companies in European processing plants, suggests a continuing growth in world woodpulp shipments, perhaps accompanied by a corresponding diminution in the proportion of non-captive market pulp entering into international trade.

CHAPTER **7** GENERAL
CONCLUSIONS

During the past decade, global consumption of paper and paperboard--the principal determinant of woodpulp demand--has increased at an average rate of around 6 per cent. Since this is roughly three times the speed at which the world's population has risen, per capita consumption has accordingly increased quite sharply too. The main influencing factor is the trend in income, and also the actual range of average income levels through which particular regions are passing. The rate of increase in consumption is very much higher as incomes rise from relatively low levels, but becomes less than proportionate at the sort of incomes which have now been reached in the United States.

The nature of this relationship between income and paper consumption means that, for a given increase in the former, the sharpest rate of expansion takes place in the developing regions. Since the pace of economic growth in such regions has also tended to be above average, they have accordingly come to account for a gradually increasing share of world consumption. On the other hand, however, the dominant position of the developed countries within total consumption is such that the absolute gap between usage in the large and the small consuming countries is still widening. Thus, the combined level of consumption in North America, Europe and the Pacific Area rose by around 65 per cent between 1954 and 1964 whereas growth in the rest of the world was between two and three times as fast. The latter, however, resulted in an absolute increase in usage of about 14.3 million tons, compared with one of well over twice this amount in the more developed regions.

These trends are expected to remain a feature of the market in the years up to 1975, and probably for some time beyond. In other words, there will be a gradual narrowing of the differential in the market shares of the more developed and the less developed regions, but a continuing widening of the gap in tonnage terms. Looking very much further ahead, however, the former tendency will ultimately lead to a reversal of the latter, which will gradually result in a more even distribution of usage on a regional basis. Since some of the

developing regions are particularly heavily populated, however,
wide disparities in per capita consumption will remain.

Looking at the period from 1964 to 1975, the combined effect
of income and population growth is expected to lead to paper consumption rising from 101.5 to 178.6 million tons, which represents
an average annual rate of growth of around 5.3 per cent. This is a
somewhat slower pace of expansion than was achieved during the
previous decade, and reflects in the main a slackening in the growth
rate in the regions which account for the bulk of consumption.

Demand for papermaking grades of woodpulp is expected to
increase at a broadly comparable rate to reach a level of around
141 million tons in 1975. Due, however, to a combination of such
factors as the bigger expansion anticipated in demand for industrial
grades of paper and paperboard than cultural papers, and the increasing use of hardwood species, consumption of chemical woodpulp in coming years is expected to increase at the fastest rate, and
the sulphate grades in particular. The relative importance of
mechanical woodpulp has already declined during 1954-64, and by
1975 its share of total woodpulp output is expected to have fallen even
further--probably to less than 25 per cent.

The gradual trend towards a slightly more even regional distribution of paper consumption is likely to be less evident as far as
woodpulp production is concerned. The five regions which were in
over-all deficit in 1964 are likely to remain so in 1975, with Europe
in particular becoming increasingly dependent on outside supplies.
Thus, the prospects are for a sharp growth in international trade,
which could well rise somewhat faster than output. Quite clearly,
the volume of aggregate inter-regional trade will expand considerably
too, stimulated by the enormous productive potential in North America
and the U.S.S.R. and shortcomings in the availability or accessibility of suitable raw materials in the remaining regions.

This assessment of probable trends in consumption and trade is
of course dependent on the realisation of adequate production levels
during the years up to 1975. It is therefore interesting to obtain
something of a glimpse into the future by means of the latest FAO
calculations of planned pulp and paper capacities, which now extend
up to the year 1970. In so doing, it is possible to get an indication
of the extent to which the seven geographical regions considered in
this study are on the way to achieving a growing level of self-
sufficiency as far as the deficit areas are concerned, or an expanding
exportable surplus in the case of North America and the U.S.S.R.

It will be recalled that a calculation was made earlier in this study of the volume of papermaking grades of woodpulp which would be required in each region in 1975. This was based on the FAO estimates of paper consumption in that year, with due allowance being made for the probable contribution made to total raw material needs by non-wood fibres and waste paper. It was, however, a purely hypothetical exercise, intended merely to indicate the magnitude of the expansion in regional output needed for self-sufficiency, rather than to imply that this would be attained. Consumption of paper is expected to increase at a very sharp pace in the deficit regions, and particularly in those where usage is low at the present time. Any proportionate reduction in its reliance on net imports, therefore, clearly means that a region must maintain an even faster rate of expansion in the provision of indigenous papermaking materials. Even where the physical availability of adequate timber resources would theoretically permit a full measure of self-sufficiency to be achieved during this period--in Latin America, for example-- problems of accessibility and, above all, the scarcity of capital will preclude its realisation. And in the case of regions less plentifully endowed with suitable species of timber, a continuing, long-term dependence on outside supplies will be inevitable.

The FAO estimates of paper consumption take account of the fact that some element of requirements in certain regions will be made up by net imports, either in the form of papermaking materials or the finished product. They also recognize that consumption in 1975 will not necessarily be equivalent to the actual level of demand prevailing in that year. The developing countries in some of the main deficit regions, for example, will not be able to permit demand to be freely exercised, in view of the consequential inroads into their limited foreign exchange earnings.

With these considerations in mind, it may now be interesting to compare the projected rate of growth in global and regional woodpulp requirements during the 1964-75 period with the increases in pulping capacity planned for the years up to 1970. Projections of future capacity installations are made each year by the FAO, and are based on a questionnaire approach to a large number of official and other sources. Although details of plans as far ahead as 1970 inevitably tend to be somewhat incomplete and thus represent an understatement of the final out-turn, this year has been selected since it may be taken as an appropriate mid-point in the eleven-year period from 1964 to 1975.

It should be stressed that the object of the calculations set out

TABLE 41

Estimates of Future Productive Capacity and Requirements of Papermaking Woodpulp

	Actual Production in 1964 (million tons)	Projected Rated Capacity in 1970 (million tons)	Estimated Domestic Requirements in 1975* (million tons)	Potential Increase 1964–70 (per cent)	Required Increase** 1970–75 (per cent)
Europe	23.5	31.0	44.2	32	43
U.S.S.R.	4.6	8.4	14.8	83	76
North America	46.2	63.0	50.4	36	–
Latin America	1.2	2.3	5.6	92	143
Africa	0.4	0.8	2.5	100	212
Asia	6.6	10.0	21.1	51	111
Pacific Area	0.9	1.4	2.3	56	64
World Total	83.4	116.9	140.9	40	21

* Based on FAO estimates of paper and paperboard consumption levels, and the assumptions made earlier in this study concerning the respective contributions likely to be made by non-wood fibre pulp and recoverable waste paper.

** This represents the increase in output necessary to achieve self-sufficiency.

in Table 41 is to illustrate broad trends and general orders of magnitude.   Hence the specific percentage figures shown should not be
taken too literally.   A number of interesting and highly significant
facts nevertheless emerge.   Looking first at global developments,
it is evident that the potential increase in output of woodpulp between
1964 and 1970, based on minimum estimates of the productive
capacity planned for installation by the end of the period, will be
somewhat ahead of world demand, if it is assumed that the latter
advances at a uniform rate.   Thus, since the table suggests that it
will be possible to raise woodpulp output by as much as 40 per cent
during the 1964-70 period, a further proportionate increase in
capacity of only about half this magnitude would be necessary in the
following five years in order to meet the level of demand anticipated
in 1975.   This would represent an average annual rate of growth of
about 4 per cent in new capacity requirements, which compares with
actual increases of around 6 per cent a year recorded during much
of the 1960's.

Viewed in absolute terms, the projected level of world capacity
by 1970 would also enable the production of much more than half of
the estimated increase in woodpulp requirements between 1964 and
1975.   The difference between actual output of woodpulp in 1964 and
the potential level of global production in 1970 amounts to as much
as 33.5 million tons, leaving a balance of only a further 24 million
tons to be produced at the end of the following five-year period.

There is, of course, an inevitable lack of precision in this outline of future planned capacity.   On the basis of the various assumptions underlying this analysis, however, the evidence nevertheless
suggests that relatively easy supply conditions will continue to
prevail in the international woodpulp market during the rest of the
present decade, and that the rate of growth in new capacity will need
to be curtailed during the early 1970's if an increasing imbalance
between supply and demand is to be avoided.

This, then, is the general global outlook, although it is interesting to note that it very largely reflects the strength of the North
American expansion in pulping capacity planned for the next few years.
It will be recalled that a relatively slow rate of advance--as distinct
from the increase in absolute terms--is expected in paper consumption
in North America during the 1964-75 period, and that the region
already produced a sizable exportable surplus in 1964.   An increase
in woodpulp output of only around 13 per cent is required, therefore
in order to achieve self-sufficiency in the mid-1970's.   Clearly a
much greater expansion will take place, since well beyond this date

North America will remain the major net supplier to the deficit regions.   An increase in woodpulp output of as much as 36 per cent (equivalent to 16.8 million tons) is already in prospect between 1964 and 1970.   Possibly the estimate is a conservative one.   Unlike the other regional figures, those projected for North American capacity at the end of this period are based on firm commitments only, and probably represent an incomplete coverage of other installation plans.

Even if no further increase in capacity occurred during the following five years, North America would still have a net exportable surplus of about 12.6 million tons of woodpulp equivalent in 1975-- compared with around 4.7 million tons in 1964.   On the other hand, if a comparable increase in capacity of a further 36 per cent were to take place between 1970 and 1975, the prospective surplus over and above estimated domestic requirements would be of the order of 35 million tons.   In all probability, North America's contribution to aggregate net regional exports in 1975 will lie somewhere between these two figures, but is perhaps more likely to be nearer the upper than the lower limit.

In the U.S.S.R., the only other net exporting region in 1964, the planned expansion in pulping capacity in the years up to 1970 is approximately in line with, or perhaps very slightly ahead of, the estimated rate of growth in woodpulp requirements throughout the 1964-75 period.   Thus a broadly comparable rate of increase in capacity is necessary during the second half of this period in order to sustain the domestic level of paper consumption anticipated in the mid-1970's.

The maintenance of a rapid rate of expansion in output of course becomes increasingly difficult as production reaches progressively higher levels.   Nevertheless, the U.S.S.R. faces no problems in finding suitable pulping material, although accessibility and competing demands on capital are a different matter.   Very extensive plans for new capacity in eastern Siberia and other parts of the region are known to be under way, however, and with some of the individual mills being among the largest in the world the proportionate effect on total capacity when they come on stream in the early 1970's will be quite significant.   It is therefore quite feasible for the expansion in Russia's woodpulp output between 1970 and 1975 to proceed at the rate of around 12 per cent a year, as implied in the last column of Table 41.   This sharp rate of growth, however, would merely serve to supply estimated domestic papermaking needs.   As the U.S.S.R. is aiming at a very substantial increase in woodpulp exports by the

mid-1970's, it will either be necessary to achieve a very much
larger expansion in production, or alternatively to restrict internal
demand for paper and paperboard to well below the level envisaged
in the FAO's estimates for 1975.

A uniform pattern emerges from the calculations set out in
Table 41 for the five deficit regions.   In each one the prospective
rate of growth in productive capacity between 1964 and 1970 is such
that a somewhat greater proportionate expansion is required during
the following five years in order to meet domestic regional requirements in 1975.   The differential between the two rates, however,
varies considerably from region to region.   In the Pacific Area
only a marginal acceleration in the growth of output is required,
although raw material limitations may be the main determining
factor here.   The latter also applies to Europe, where a more
substantial shortfall is emerging, particularly when viewed in
tonnage terms.   Elsewhere, Africa and Asia would need to achieve
an expansion in woodpulp output between 1970 and 1975 equivalent to
rather more than double the rate of growth which is in prospect
during the 1964-70 period in order to realise a state of self-sufficiency,
while in Latin America a 50 per cent quickening in the pace of expansion would be required.

On the basis of this broad assessment, therefore, it seems quite
clear that, in the period up to 1975, Europe (to an increasing extent),
Latin America, Africa, Asia, and the Pacific Area (possibly to a
declining extent) will in aggregate remain fairly heavily dependent on
net imports of woodpulp, or paper and paperboard.   The imports
will be supplied mainly by North America but probably to an increasing extent by the U. S. S. R. during the course of the 1970's.

It is possible to shed some further light on the form which this
trade flow is perhaps likely to take by comparing the relative expansion plans for pulp and paper capacity in the main producing regions.
Looking first at the U. S. S. R., the projections compiled by the FAO
do not reveal any marked shift in emphasis towards either pulp or
paper capacity in the years up to 1970.   Planned increases in
capacity in both sectors are expected to be pretty much in line at a
rate of between 7 and 9 per cent a year.   A similar trend has in
fact been evident since 1960, but it is particularly significant that
pulp capacity has been, and is expected to remain, broadly equivalent to papermaking capacity.   In each of the other regions, on the
other hand, woodpulp capacity falls short of papermaking capacity
by anything up to 30 per cent, and by about 20 per cent in the world
as a whole.   The balance is made up by other papermaking materials,

and since these also make an important contribution in the U. S. S. R.
it is evident that the capacity for producing woodpulp in this region
is being maintained at a level well above the domestic paper industry's
requirements.   Paper output is,if anything,falling short of what is
needed to sustain the rate of advance in domestic consumption envisaged by the FAO for the 1964-75 period.   Thus it seems likely
that virtually all of the increase in Russia's exports in coming years
will take the form of woodpulp rather than pulp-based products.

In Western Europe, however, a completely different pattern
emerges from a consideration of relative trends in pulp and paper
capacity.   Throughout the 1960's there has been a consistent and,
in fact, a widening gulf between capacity in the two sectors, with
the annual rate of expansion in pulping capacity likely to be at least
1 per cent lower than the growth in papermaking capacity during the
latter part of the decade.   As there is little scope for raising waste
paper's proportionate contribution to total fibrous requirements, the
inevitable conclusion to be drawn is that, in net terms, Europe will
become increasingly dependent on external sources of woodpulp
supply.   Furthermore, there are signs of a growing trend towards
vertical integration in the Nordic countries.   Intra-European trade
in woodpulp may therefore tend to diminish in relative importance.
As such, the needs of the papermaking industry in the main deficit
areas--the U. K. and the EEC countries--will tend to be increasingly
felt in the U. S. S. R. and North America.

The projected development of pulp and paper capacity in North
America merely serves to substantiate the general conclusions which
have already emerged from this study.   A very significant narrowing in the differential between capacity in the two sectors has in fact
occurred since 1960.   Moreover, this trend is expected to continue
for the rest of the decade. to the point where the prospective level
of woodpulp output falls short of papermaking capacity by only about
5 million tons--or around 8 per cent.   Other fibrous raw materials,
and in particular a very high utilisation of waste paper,will help to
close the gap, but to a large extent the deficit regions will continue
to look to North America to produce a growing woodpulp surplus to
meet their increasing demands.

A major part of these will come from the U. K. , the EEC
countries and Japan.   The less advanced deficit countries, however,
will clearly be unable to use a rapidly increasing element of their
foreign exchange earnings on imports of either pulp or paper.   It
will be necessary to cover at least a substantial part of their growing
requirements by the establishments of indigenous production facilities.
Not only is such a development desirable--it is in fact essential if

such areas are to be assured of adequate supplies.   During the next
decade, and for some time beyond, there is unlikely to be any undue
pressure imposed on the timber resources of the two surplus regions
in supplying world needs.   Looking somewhat further ahead, however,
a continuation of the growth in demand in both the developed and the
developing countries may ultimately place something of a strain even
on the physical capacity of regions as plentifully endowed as North
America and the U. S. S. R.

ABOUT THE AUTHOR

R. L. J. Carter is Deputy Research Director of the Commodities Division at The Economist Intelligence Unit Ltd. (EIU) in London. A graduate of the London School of Economics and Political Science, Mr. Carter has traveled extensively throughout the world. He is a member of the Market Research Society, has contributed to a number of EIU publications, and has written many specialized studies dealing with the pulp and paper industry. Before joining EIU he worked for the New Zealand Meat Producers' Board in London.